EXPERIENCING ENDINGS
AND BEGINNINGS

EXPERIENCING ENDINGS AND BEGINNINGS

Isca Salzberger-Wittenberg

KARNAC

First published in 2013 by
Karnac Books Ltd
118 Finchley Road
London NW3 5HT

British Library Cataloguing in Publication Data

A C.I.P. for this book is available from the British Library

ISBN-13: 978-1-78049-171-4

Typeset by V Publishing Solutions Pvt Ltd., Chennai, India

Printed in Great Britain

www.karnacbooks.com

& over-coming emotional & developmental tensions in early life.

For my children Raphael and Jonathan and grandchildren Gideon, Daniel, Amos, Libbi, and Kadya

CONTENTS

ACKNOWLEDGEMENTS

My deepest feelings of gratitude are to my parents who provided me with a secure childhood, a home embodying religious ideals, and a rich cultural life.

I am indebted to the analytic teachers at the Tavistock, especially to Dugmore Hunter, John Bowlby, Esther Bick, and Martha Harris. I am grateful to the supervisors of my clinical work: Esther Bick, Isabel Menzies, and Donald Meltzer who greatly enriched my understanding of my work with patients. I feel deeply grateful to my analysts Sonny Davidson and Wilfred Bion for developing my understanding of myself and encouraging me to follow my intuition, frequently revealed in my dreams. I wish to thank the many patients who helped to widen my experience of emotional pain and how to struggle with it; I also want to thank the many students whose challenging questions encouraged me to clarify my ideas.

I have for a long time had the wish to write about experiences of endings and beginnings and to extend the psychoanalytic understanding of human relationships to include the spiritual aspect of human beings, so closely linked to the belief that life is meaningful. Neville Symington's book "Emotion and Spirit" and our ongoing correspondence inspired me to think further about the need to bring together what he calls, "the core values of the world's religions" and the psychoanalytic understanding of the mind.

The writing of this book began many years ago, was often interrupted for long periods, but received an impetus from a small group of colleagues who met to study ancient wisdoms such as the Kabbalah and to read the works of modern spiritual-religious writers. We looked at the actions of outstanding leaders, as well as those of ordinary people, who embody their love of mankind and view the resolution of conflict between different nations and religions as an essential part of their life's work.

I owe very particular thanks to two people from this original group. Ricky Emanuel and Helen Muller met with me on a monthly basis over the last eighteen months to read the drafts of the chapters I was writing for this book. Their constructive criticism, their knowledge and insights, their support in keeping me to task, have been invaluable.

I am grateful to Kate Stratton for her careful editorial support.

I am very grateful to Oliver Rathbone, Director of Karnac Books, for his encouragement and eagerness to see the completed manuscript.

ABOUT THE AUTHOR

Isca Salzberger-Wittenberg is a consultant psychoanalytic psychotherapist for children and adults who has worked at the Tavistock Clinic for twenty-five years and was vice-chairman of the Tavistock for ten years. She was a senior tutor in the clinical training of child psychotherapists, has led infant observation seminars in London for fifty years, and trained analysts and psychologists in Vienna and Oslo in infant observation. She has lectured and run seminars in Austria, Germany, Italy, Norway, Spain, and Sweden, and run workshops in Australia and South Africa. She has held temporary professorships at the universities of Turin and Klagenfurt.

She now works primarily in private practice, doing brief and long-term psychotherapy. She has been made a lifetime honorary member of the senior staff of the Tavistock Clinic where she still does some teaching as well as facilitating experiential groups. She has published many articles in professional journals, contributed chapters to a number of psychoanalytic books (including two on autism), and written two books: *Psycho-Analytic Insight and Relationships: A Kleinian Approach* (translated into nine languages) and *The Emotional Experience of Learning and Teaching*—the latter including contributions by Gianna Williams and Elsie Osborne, and which has been translated into eight languages.

PREFACE

In her late eighties, Isca Wittenberg's mind is young. It is such a pity we have to die when the mind is still developing. Couldn't we instruct the body to wait until the mind has reached the end of its journey? No doubt the body would reply: "Well, when it comes to Isca Wittenberg I would have to keep going, like Methuselah, until 969 years of age." What is so heartening about this book about endings and beginnings is Isca's frank admission that only lately (giving hope to those of us who have not yet reached eighty) has she realised that her own shocking upheaval in the event of Hitler's tyranny, which brought to an end a peaceful life in Germany and the start of life in England as an "enemy alien", so focused her mind upon endings and beginnings.

She teaches us that a new environment stimulates into life a new mental state within us. Recent research has confirmed this.[1] The failure to adapt the mind to the new circumstance always has consequences either great or small, and even the small are not so small once we examine the whole situation carefully. We often don't realise that we have moved from one environment to another. We go so often from home to work that we may not take in what a huge transition that is. It is also very alarming to realise that, in response to a new environment, a quite different person emerges. We are all multiple personalities. What Isca does is to draw our attention to these changed environments and by bringing these into awareness we then establish a continuity at a deeper level within ourselves. Awareness always implies that an aspect of the mind is embracing the flow of changes that are occurring. It was Martin Buber who pointed out that causality

> … is no unbroken sequence but an ever new flashing forth of power and moving out towards its production; it is a volcanic movement without continuity …[2]

and he goes on to say that continuity is achieved through the agency of a "magic power". Isca, as witness to us in this book, has this magic power that enables her to be acutely aware of the changed environments.

In this investigation Isca travels from the womb to death. There are so many beginnings and endings. The baby ends his life in the womb and is suddenly cast into a frightening new environment. Isca draws on her enormous experience both of infant observation and of treating young children in psychoanalysis. Of course she not only treats children and adolescents but also adults. She gives the most illustrative cases and shows how the behaviour of young babies differs hugely, as is also true of her adult cases. She shows how mothers manage the very different emotional behaviour of their newborn babies. Just as no adult couple is the same as any other so, too, no two mother-baby couples are ever the same. But Isca draws attention to another dimension. She emphasises that the baby is not only drawn lovingly to her mother but also that the baby is drawn to something beyond. In a letter which she wrote to me six years ago, after I had sent her a paper about reverence of children for their parents, she said:

> My feeling is that dependence does include fear as well as love but reverence implies an awareness of goodness which starts at the baby's wonder at mother's goodness … I believe that the baby of a few months, looking at mother adoringly, is aware that she contains something that is both hers but also not hers—an endowment which has been given.

In this way she is again in tune with Martin Buber's view that the baby, from the earliest year, in the womb even, stretches out beyond mother to the whole world. It is that "beyond" that captivates Isca's soul. It is reminiscent of that remarkable man Macneile Dixon who, in the Gifford Lectures in 1935, said:

> The first and fundamental wonder is existence itself. That I should be alive, conscious, a person, a part of the whole, that I should have emerged out of nothingness, that the Void should have given birth not merely to things, but to me. Among the many millions who throughout the centuries have crossed the stage of time probably not more than a handful have looked about them with astonishment, or found their own presence within the visible scene in any way surprising.[3]

It is this vision which characterises the spiritual dimension. So much of our thinking within the social sciences, within psychology, within psychoanalysis, is rooted in the assumption that the purpose of living is the struggle for survival, that it takes Isca to take us out of this. In this way she is in the tradition of Viktor Frankl, Macneile Dixon, and Tolstoy, who all thought that there was in life a purpose higher than the struggle for survival.

There is an underlying theme to all Isca's essays in this book: the spiritual dimension that underpins human experience. It is very significant that she places the spiritual not as something aside from human experience but as something within it. This is so important that, unless emphasised, it could be missed. The spiritual is not something aside from human communication and experience but *in* it.

In these chapters she treats young children, watches with care and concern the reactions of babies to being weaned and their mothers' experience of weaning, listens to elderly men and women who have retired from work, talks to the very old who are edging towards the gateway of death. In all these cases Isca helps these people not only to accept their changed situation in life but to see fresh opportunities and purposes in the new environment in which they find themselves. As one looks to see what it is that Isca has done to help them, there does not at first glimpse appear to be any amazing new insights or profound psychological intuitions. So what is it that Isca has done? I think it is quite simple: she is sympathetic to the pain of those who approach her for help. She listens and offers sympathetic understanding, and this helps the person who has approached her. She is in touch with pain. Listening to these accounts which Isca shares with us gives conviction to a truth that has been known by wise people for centuries: that a pain shared, a pain that is understood, does not remove the pain but heals the soul. But why? Because the sufferer is no longer on his own, or her own, but in a shared communion with others. It does not mean that Isca just listens and that the patient's pain is the same as her own. If this were true it would be a disaster for the patient because then he or she would be moulded into the contours of another's pain. It is that Isca is able to see into the particular pain of this person who has approached her for help. She can only do this because she is able to experience her own pain, to step aside from the particularity that is hers and see the pain of the other. She does not think that her pain is the same as the other's pain but her own pain—and her reflection upon it—enables her to see the pain of the other. It is her ability to reflect upon it that is healing for the patient.

It is because Isca is able to know her own pain, then stand outside of it as an observer and see that this is *her* pain and not the pain of anyone else, that she is able to see the other as other, and the other's pain as his or her pain. The root, however, of her understanding comes from her own self-knowledge and it is knowledge of her pain and not of anyone else's that enables her to see into the particular pain of the other.

This ancient wisdom is confirmed by the fact that Isca frequently throws her own experiences into this book. So one senses that when people approach her, they do not feel that here is someone superior to them, someone who will listen patronisingly, but rather someone who is also in the human community and has suffered and suffers just as much as the patient or maybe more. It is not that she tells them her own experiences but that they sense she is their equal. The patient then no longer feels an alienated being but rather one in the midst of life, someone in the human community. A shared pain is a pain that has had the poison siphoned out of it.

This brings me back to what I have said about the spiritual dimension, which is central to her vision of life. This sense of a shared communion implies that there is knowledge that life is more than a struggle for survival; that life has a purpose that goes beyond the practical necessities for survival. She tells of the sad case of a man whom she was able to help whose twenty-three-year-old grandson was killed in a car crash. No one can take away the tragedy of an event like this. Our human lives are studded with disasters that are outside our control. The spiritual dimension teaches us that life, even in the midst of such tragedies, has meaning. This is something that Viktor Frankl managed to hold onto even in the most dire of human circumstances when he was in the concentration camp.[4] Isca did not suffer this, the most horrific torture and shame of our generation, but she was close to it. Her father was in one for a short while. So, like Frankl, she did not become bitter or cynical but lived instead knowing that pain is part of life, managed to embrace it in herself, and so then those who sought her help sensed that here was someone who was able to endow them with new hope for their changed circumstances.

Neville Symington

Notes

1. See Brooks, D. (2011). The Social Animal: The Hidden Sources of Love, Character and Achievement. New York: Random House.
2. Buber, M. (1937). I and Thou pp. 35–36. Translated by Ronald Gregor Smith. Second Edition, (1958) with a postscript by the author. Edinburgh: T. and T. Clark.
3. Macneile Dixon, W. (1958). The Human Situation pp. 72–73. Harmondsworth: Penguin.
4. Frankl, V. (1962). Man's Search for Meaning. London: Hodder & Stoughton.

AUTHOR'S NOTE

Much of the clinical work described goes back over very many years; it has therefore not been possible to contact and thank all of those patients I have worked with. I do want to express how deeply indebted I feel to them for enriching my experience.

I have used the male pronoun when writing more generally, and changed names when giving descriptions of the clinical material in order to preserve confidentiality.

I have used the term "projection" in parts of the text although the correct psychoanalytic term for the mechanism involved is "projective identification" (the omnipotent phantasy of being able to split off, temporarily get rid of, parts of one's personality and put them into another person or, alternatively, to communicate unbearable anxiety; for instance the baby is able to act in a way that engenders in the mother feelings he does not want to have or which he wants his mother to have and respond to). The mechanism may be used by persons of any age in relation to another. I have used the term "projection" in the text as this may be less confusing for the lay readership.

Wishing to bring as many illustrations as possible, I have mainly chosen examples from brief interventions. Being able to do such brief therapeutic work effectively is, however, dependent on engaging in intensive, long-term psychoanalytic work.

CHAPTER ONE

Learning from experience of endings and beginnings

I have for many years been impressed by the intensity and depth of emotions aroused by beginnings and endings: ending one phase of life and entering a new one, the beginning and the ending of a course of study, becoming part of an organisation and leaving it, starting a new relationship, and ending an old one—life is full of beginnings and endings, constantly facing us with having to deal with change. This book is the result of reflections, based on my professional and personal experiences of the emotional turmoil to which such changes give rise and the ways in which different individuals and groups try to deal with them.

We tend to associate endings with fear and dread. But there are exceptions. For instance, the ending of a miserable, restricting marriage may bring relief; a person who is in constant agonising pain, progressively disabled, may long for her life to end; leaving a country where one is persecuted is a life-saving event. Beginnings tend to be associated with hope and excitement. But there again it is not necessarily so. For instance, having to do a further course of training in order to be employable may be dreaded; being promoted to a senior job may be looked forward to but the responsibility that goes with it may be feared.

Endings and beginnings are intimately linked. Every ending requires us to come to terms with what we have lost and to begin anew. Most beginnings involve having to let go of some aspect of the life, and/or the views on life, that we held before. Getting married, having a baby, acquiring a new house, starting a course of study, a new job, embarking on a new venture, all these events beckon, promising us a richer, happier, more fulfilling life. It is the hope invested in new experiences that makes us look forward to them and to seek them out. Yet the German saying, "*Aller Anfang ist schwer*", ("Every beginning is difficult") draws attention to the fact that starting something new may also be difficult and make us anxious. We may wonder whether we can live up to what is expected of us, not knowing whether we have the physical, mental/emotional capacities needed to deal with the new situation. And while we may wish to get away from what we find unsatisfactory, limiting, frustrating, uninteresting in the present and wish to widen our experience, to learn, explore, create, embark on something new, there remains the uncertainty about whether the new experience will in fact live up to what we desire. Will the baby we long for be beautiful or deformed, will it enrich our lives or rob us of the freedom we enjoy now; will the new house be built on solid foundations; will the new job, the new course of study be disappointing, boring; will the new partner be loving and lovable or too difficult to live with, will we be happier or is it better to remain single and preserve our independence?

Before we embark on any new venture, we weigh up whether it is worth taking the risk to face the as yet unknown. In spite of all the limitations and frustrations in our present life, sticking to the same routine, the same way of conducting our individual and institutional life may feel easier, a safer option. The saying, "Better the devil you know than the one you don't know", gives expression to the feeling that however uncomfortable and unsatisfactory our present state, at least it is known, while the unknown holds the potential of danger, making us fearful, sometimes even terrified. We have somehow managed up to now but how will we fare if we open ourselves to a new experience, a new challenge, new knowledge? Change is threatening; it needs faith, hope, and courage to embrace the new experience.

Most beginnings require us not only to let go of what we are familiar with but also to relinquish something that we value or some advantage associated with the previous state. But do we actually have any choice? Only to some extent, for beginnings and endings are an inevitable concomitant of moving through the life cycle: leaving the relative safety of intrauterine existence and beginning life in the outer world, moving from babyhood to becoming a child, giving up the advantages of being the baby; and as we grow up, reach adolescence and adulthood, we have to let go of some of the privileges of being a child and take on the responsibilities that go with becoming an adult. Our relationship with a partner undergoes many adjustments and having a child brings about a major change. The relationship between parents and their offspring also demands constant change, some letting go as the children grow up, leave home, get married, have children of their own. We may look forward to the gains that we hope will accompany every new stage of development yet at the same time some good aspect of the previous phase may have to be relinquished. These losses are likely to make us anxious and angry at times when we might expect—and when others might expect us—to be happy. Resentment at what has to be given up may seriously interfere with the enjoyment of what the new step we have taken may have to offer.

There are also events in life that are primarily marked by loss: being separated, parting from those we love and/or rely on, illness that leaves us with less physical and/or mental powers; loss of work, ageing, bereavement, facing the end of our life. All these endings arouse such dread that they are seldom spoken of or even thought about. Yet being able to be aware of and to face these losses allows us to some extent to prepare ourselves mentally and emotionally. If we avoid doing so, it makes us even more prone to being overwhelmed by panic when the dreaded event actually occurs. We may feel ashamed of the emotional turmoil we find ourselves in, be reluctant to admit it to ourselves and inclined to try to run away from it. Alternatively, we might be over-whelmed by our painful, disturbing emotional state but fear that there is no one who can tolerate our fears, our anger, grief, depression, despair. All this may make us reluctant to communicate, to share our feelings with others. There may indeed be no partner, no friend, no colleague willing to listen, for many people are afraid that they will be "infected" by another person's painful emotional state. Much suffering therefore goes on silently, with individuals being left to manage their pain on their own, making it all the harder for them to bear. We may try to run away from the pain of loss but unless we are able to mourn what we have lost or are about to lose, we will not be able to internalise/preserve within ourselves what has been of value in the past; nor will we be able to build on what we have gained from the past experience and enjoy what is still available to us in the new situation.

We tend to underestimate how powerfully seemingly ordinary beginnings and endings may affect us. As I shall say a great deal about the emotional states evoked by beginnings in the following chapter, I would like to consider here how the disturbing experience of what might be considered an ordinary ending was brought home to me on a brief visit to Australia, some forty years ago. I had been invited for a fortnight to lead seminars for psychiatrists, psychotherapists, social workers, clergy, and general medical practitioners in Brisbane. I requested that in the first week participants bring examples of cases they had recently started seeing while in the second week the focus would be on separation and ending work with their patients/clients.

Most members of the conference showed intense interest and worked hard, clearly desiring to get as much out of this learning opportunity as possible. At times I drew attention to the fact that the clients' emotional experience at beginning and ending was also likely to be felt by members of the conference both at the start of our relationship and now as it drew to an end. I shared the group's sense that the conference had been useful and that it had gone well. However, when I entered the meeting on the last day, I was immediately struck by the very different atmosphere that pervaded the room. Members were silent, their posture indicating that they were withdrawing into themselves; some looked angry, some utterly miserable, and some faces bore a vacant expression. They reminded me of children left too long on their own, being so angry that they project their pain, unable or unwilling to verbalise their feelings. Eventually, someone said: "We want a book next time, not someone who goes away and leaves us after a fortnight." I talked about the disappointment and anger at our time together having come to an end but this did nothing to dispel or lighten the hostility and heaviness that members were clearly feeling. The enormous bouquet of flowers I was handed at the end of the meeting felt to me like a wreath for my grave rather than a gift of appreciation. I felt utterly devastated, guilty and despairing at leaving the group in such a state. I was afraid that their anger at my leaving would lead members of the group to inwardly destroy the work we had done together; that all we had learnt would be lost, their efforts and mine wasted; I feared I might even have left them in a worse state than they had been in before my visit.

The reports I subsequently received from the organiser of the conference seemed to bear this out. There was much fighting between the various professional groups and anger directed at the psychiatrist who had invited me. I blamed myself for not having given enough thought to the ending and for not having prepared them, or myself, for it. I felt that I should have known from my clinical work and from feeling bereft myself at ending even brief engagements, how very painful it is to part, especially when it has been an emotionally intense and precious time. I should have known how essential it is to give time and space to face and share the feelings of frustration, anger, despair, and loneliness to which endings give rise. No doubt the very great expectations put upon me as a visiting teacher from overseas—and at that time such visits were a very rare occurrence—gave an extra edge to the disappointment at my leaving.

I resolved there and then that in future I would pay greater attention to exploring endings with students on any course for which I was responsible. I also determined to try to look at beginnings and endings within organisations, especially in my own place of work, the Tavistock Clinic. I was fortunate to be allowed to introduce experiential groups as part of the Clinic's introductory event, giving newcomers the opportunity to reflect on and share what they felt at starting their training with us; those who had come from overseas naturally found the beginning especially difficult. I also started a weekly endings seminar in which we discussed ending psychotherapy/analysis with patients whom the students were treating. We looked at how different patients were feeling at ending therapy and at the emotions ending aroused in the therapist, especially if treatment was ended prematurely. It soon became evident that those students who were approaching the end of their training, and therefore leaving the Clinic, were finding it very difficult to be faced with the double task of coping with their patients' anger at being left and their own feelings about ending their time with us. As one student put it: "I would like to be able to say to my patients: don't blame me for leaving you, blame the Tavistock for getting rid of me." Eventually, the professional committee also allowed me to hold an annual institutional ending event at which students and staff who were approaching the end of their time at the Clinic could share their thoughts and feelings about leaving, losing the support of their peer group, their teachers, and the organisation, as well as the pleasure at having qualified and being able to work elsewhere. For a long time I could only find one other permanent staff member, the senior psychologist Elsie Osborne, willing to join me in this new venture. Even after I had retired, students for some years asked for an ending event and the chairman of the Clinic would write to me, asking whether I would be willing to run it—of course, I was and was glad to do so. After a few years, some other permanent staff members became interested in taking it over and the annual ending event eventually became part of the Tavistock Clinic's regular programme.

I was relieved, in fact thrilled, to be given another chance, two years after the first workshop, to work with the Brisbane group again. This time I structured the conference differently. I was aware that it had been a mistake for me to have led every session. Instead, I asked psychiatrists within the membership to lead the work discussion groups (with ten people in each group) and told them that I was going to lead the plenary meetings for the total membership of fifty people. At the opening plenary, I was asked what I had felt at the end of the previous conference and I thought it useful to give an honest answer. One female psychiatrist had the courage to say that she had not felt any hostility towards me when I left last time but suddenly, on my return, felt in such a state of fury with me that she could hardly get herself to the conference room. Others voiced how awful the ending of the last conference had been. It was very helpful to begin facing such angry emotions openly right from the start. I spoke about how hard it might be for members to get deeply involved again, knowing that we would have to part at the end of two weeks. I told the group that I thought there was a possibility that if we could keep the ending in mind and share our feelings about it, it might not come as such a shock as previously.

We had daily staff meetings: one in the morning and one at the end of the day. Every evening I studied the reports on what had been discussed in the work discussion groups. At first, the cases members had chosen to present were about mothers neglecting their children, mothers deserting the family, cruel mothers, abused children, children needing to be fostered. It was a revelation: it was obvious that the cases they had brought mirrored what they felt about me, the cruel mother of the conference. I put the main themes raised in the work discussion groups on the blackboard so that everyone could see them as they came into the plenary sessions. Before starting to talk about clinical work and looking at useful concepts, the relationship of members to me, the cruel mother who had abandoned them last time and would be leaving them again after a fortnight, was the subject of close scrutiny right from the beginning. Soon other topics, either arising from the work discussion groups or from incidents that happened during the course of the conference, were spoken about and followed through by looking at how learning from our own emotional experience might help us to be in touch with what our patients/clients were experiencing. This time the ending was thought about, prepared for, worked at. (For a fuller description of the work, see Salzberger-Wittenberg, 1978.)

Although we all felt the end to be painful—indeed, in some ways more so than the last time—it was far less hurtful. Having fully faced the frustration and anger, we were able to arrive at feeling sad and grateful for the very emotive experiences we had shared, all summarised in a moving poem written by one of the members. Our meetings had indeed taught us all a great deal (I, of course, shared with the group how much I had learnt from this and the previous conference). Our learning had enriched us all and could be nourished within us, thus forming the basis for further enrichment of our hearts and minds. The clinicians within the group agreed to have a follow-up a month after I had left and at that meeting they decided to found the Brisbane Psychotherapy Association. I felt encouraged to work more than ever in the "here and now" with groups of students as well as to run experiential groups for educational psychologists in training at the Tavistock Clinic.

It may seem strange—as indeed it did to me—that it was only very many years later that it dawned on me that my interest, my sensitive awareness of endings and beginnings, was likely to be due to my own dramatic experiences of having had to leave Germany—where I was born and spent my childhood and early adolescence—and to begin life anew in England. I was nine years old when Hitler came to power. Jewish people in prestigious positions lost their jobs; books by Jewish authors were destroyed. Persecution of Jewish people increased year by year; Jewish children were excluded from attending state schools. Fortunately there were two excellent Jewish schools in Frankfurt, my hometown, but on our way to school we were waylaid and regularly spat at by state school children. I knew not to open my mouth when I saw placards of derogatory pictures and slogans about Jews displayed at street corners for I was aware that it would land me in very serious trouble. My best friend was Hannelore, a Christian girl living in the apartment above us, but her family later had to move out, as it was forbidden for Jews and non-Jews to mix; I never saw or heard from Hannelore again. Quite a number of Jewish families emigrated but many stayed, not able to believe that a man like Hitler would be tolerated by such a civilised, highly cultured society. Others remained because they were unable to obtain a visa to another country or did not want to be parted from old or disabled relatives.

There were more and more prohibitions and attacks on Jews. I could not understand why so many adults remained hopeful that things would change for the better. My father, though aware of our precarious position, felt that as rabbi of a large congregation, he needed to stay to look after his distressed congregants. He declared: "The captain is the last person to leave a sinking ship." And then, all hell broke loose on the night of 9 November 1938, subsequently called *Kristallnacht*, the Night of Broken Glass—because all Jewish shops and department stores were broken into as well as other Jewish properties, including the youth centre right next to our house. My father was called early in the morning to witness the burning of his synagogue and also another at which he had officiated. This was followed by the hunting down of all Jewish men—in our town and throughout Germany—who were carted off to concentration camps. Many soon perished, either shot or beaten to death or dying from sepsis following frost-bite, the result of having to stand in thin prison clothes outside the barracks for many hours in the freezing cold winter nights. One of my teachers died that way. I anxiously looked out of the window each day, hoping that the postman was not carrying a small, wooden box, for that was the way the ashes of the deceased were delivered to their families. Nazi youths broke into our flat in the night, shouting: "Now for the first time in your life you children will learn to do work." I was so sure that we were to be taken to a concentration camp that I started to put on my clothes. Instead we were marched into my father's study and made to throw the Hebrew books from our third floor flat into the yard below.

We learnt that it was possible to get men released from concentration camp (unlike later, when war had broken out) if one could show evidence that one was about to get a visa and would leave Germany within a short time. My mother immediately phoned friends from all over the world and within fourteen days a telegram arrived offering my father a position as rabbi of a congregation in Los Angeles. My mother rushed with it to the Gestapo (Nazi secret service) and a week later my father came home, hardly recognisable and suffering from double pneumonia. He would not have survived another day or two in the camp. There followed another four months of waiting for temporary visas to enter Britain (due to the quota system applied by the USA we would have had to wait years to obtain an American visa). My father had to report to the Gestapo every week, was shouted at and threatened with being sent back to Dachau concentration camp because we had not yet left Germany. What sustained me at this time was my mother's courage and my father's faith.

On Easter Monday 1939 we were at last able to fly to England, taking with us a few suitcases and ten shillings each—and my cello—which was all we were allowed. The loss of our possessions was of minor importance; the great thing was that we had survived! We were welcomed by friends of my parents with whom we then stayed for a few weeks. I was impressed by the helpful policemen, the "bobbies", who spared no effort to help if one did not find one's way. But I was amazed to discover how ignorant people were about what was happening in Germany. For instance, when someone at the bus stop asked me where I had come from and I told them, some responded saying: "Oh, I so admire the Germans, they are so efficient." However, once war broke out, all German and Austrian refugees became "enemy aliens". When my parents were interviewed by a selection board to decide what category of refugee we fitted into, an officer told my father: "Surely, if you had worn your dog collar [as vicars do but rabbis don't] they would not have taken you to a concentration camp." After the fall of France, which meant that Britain was now in great peril of being invaded, many thousands of refugees (as well as some real enemy aliens) were interned on the Isle of Man while some were shipped to Canada or Australia. However, after three months it was realised that treating harmless refugees in this way had been a mistake and people were gradually released and brought back from overseas. Many actively joined the battle against Nazi Germany. We were full of admiration for Churchill, the bravery of the air force, and the resilience and sense of humour of ordinary British people in the face of day and night bombings—and eternally grateful to Britain for saving us and the world from Hitler's, and his allies', brutality.

After a short while my father, who had not been interned, was elected to become the rabbi of a German and Austrian refugee congregation, my eldest sister had a scholarship to study in Glasgow, and my middle sister was sent to Jewish school in the South to help dig a swimming pool, no easy job. When asked by the Jewish committee dealing with refugees what I wanted to do, I said I would like to work with babies and children and was sent to a training centre for nursery nurses. I was very unhappy there. The matron of the home for orphaned children greeted me, saying that I had to work harder than the other girls, as the committee had persuaded her to admit me at half the normal fee. We were not allowed to pick up crying babies and they were only fed on a strict four-hourly schedule; it was heart-breaking. I also felt lonely, as I had nothing in common with the other girls who were interested in make-up and boyfriends while my mind was preoccupied with what had happened to us such a short time ago and with worries about all the members of the family and friends left behind in Germany. My mother wrote saying that I should give the training a month and if I was still as homesick, I could come back to London. But by that time I had fallen in love with a three-year-old little boy with a heart defect and did not feel I could leave him. So I stayed for the year-long training but turned down the offer to stay on as a staff nurse. My sister Ruth and I then went to work at a war-time nursery in Hemel Hempstead, not far from Boxmoor, where, together with my parents, we had been offered rooms in a mansion belonging to a very kind, English, Christian couple. (Mr Micklem, a real English gentleman, had been a Queen's Counsellor in Queen Victoria's time). They called us in every evening to have tea with them and listen to the news—as enemy aliens we were not allowed to own a radio.

In 1943, the Jewish Aid Committee sponsored a scholarship for me to study social science at Birmingham University. I was asked to stay in a hostel in town or at the Quaker College. Up until then I had felt an unwanted alien but Woodbrooke, with its Quaker community, welcomed me with open arms. The fact that I came from another country and belonged to a different religious faith was, if anything, regarded as an asset. Everyone was appreciated, whatever their background. For the first time in many years I felt I could be myself—and I flourished in this warm, calm, cheerful, peaceful atmosphere. My experiences at Woodbrooke linked to the constant Jewish prayer for peace amongst the nations and my father's interest in all religions. In the early 1930s he used to travel to London to attend meetings of the World Congress of Faiths, founded by Sir Francis Younghusband.

With hindsight, I feel that my experiences in Nazi Germany, and beginning life anew in Britain, not only made me sensitively aware of all endings but influenced my life in a number of ways. Because I could not comprehend how our good German friends could become our enemies, I felt a need to understand more about human nature and this eventually led me to psychoanalysis and to becoming an analytic psychotherapist. Having been treated as an outcast made me wish to build bridges: between members of different professions, between different religions, as well as trying to bridge the gap between the broad-minded spiritual-religious orientation gained in childhood and the psychoanalytic insights acquired in adulthood. The latter taught me that as well as trying to avoid what is painful by blaming others, we tend to project into others the unwanted, destructive aspects of ourselves. Such divisiveness/splitting leads to fraught relationships in our personal lives and fights between groups. On a larger scale, it can lead to attacks on foreigners, immigrants, other races, other religions, and to genocide. As well as the commandment to "Love thy neighbour as thyself", the Hebrew Bible also contains the commandment to "Love the stranger that sojourns with thee … you shall love him as thyself, for you were strangers in the land of Egypt." This love is only achievable if one is capable of identifying with the stranger, seeing the common humanity as well as respecting differences, instead of attributing feared and painful experiences to the stranger.

At every turn, as Bion (1962b) says, we have to choose whether to avoid emotional pain or to face it; to live with lies, or to live with truth, which he calls "the food that nourishes the mind". In my professional and social encounters I am constantly impressed by the almost universal avoidance of facing endings. Even asking my group of teachers to consider what it feels like to approach the end of their course at the Tavistock Clinic is usually met with the response that surely this is not the right time to think about it: it is felt to be either too early or too late to do so; in other words, thinking about it is to be avoided. Yet it is well known that there are drop-outs and much absenteeism towards the end of any course of study. After introducing a meeting about ending at the beginning of the third term of the one-year course, absenteeism was no longer a problem. In fact, many students resolved to use this last term to get help with problems they had not previously had the courage to discuss but now felt that they needed to face, before it was too late.

At leaving parties the past is celebrated, speeches praise the person who is leaving: there is no mention of anger (or glee) nor of sadness; these feelings are not spoken about but are often enacted. Here is what happened to one of my friends: she was very highly regarded and loved by everyone in the organisation where she worked. When she was leaving her job, her colleagues arranged a wonderful farewell party in her honour but when she got to the place designated on the invitation, she found that no one was there—they had forgotten to tell her that they had changed the venue! It was she who was to feel deserted.

The dread evoked by even ordinary endings becomes understandable if we realise that they stir up fears of the loss of security, of being abandoned, left to die.

These powerful feelings stem from earliest infancy, the time when our life of being carried within the womb comes to an end, and the cord that connected us to mother is cut. Equally, our excitement and anxieties at beginnings has its roots in the experience of the newborn opening his eyes to a whole new world, one that as well as being terrifyingly unfamiliar, is also full of wonder and beauty.

I believe that human beings have, from the very beginning of life, a need and capacity to seek connections. The newborn, cut off at birth from the physical connection with mother, the source of his life, seeks to reconnect to the mother's body and her resources. With mother's help and understanding, he uses his sensual and mental equipment to gradually explore and understand what he encounters outside and within himself. The anger and anxiety caused by being weaned needs to be understood and the baby helped to see that mother is still available and loves him. The child gradually becomes aware of wider connections, the interdependence of mother and father, of the family and others in the outside world, and, at some later date, of human life and the environment.

As we grow, our horizon expands. We may find meaningful connections between our experience and those of others and bring together different areas of knowledge and beliefs. Eventually we may reach out to wonder about the mysteries that are beyond science and seek to comprehend how our love, our creativity, as well as our destructiveness, is linked to such forces within the universe. It is the linking of good experiences in the past, present, and future, of something within and beyond ourselves, and the discovery of meaningful connections, which drives us—in spite of the fear of what we might discover—to go on exploring the outer world and trying to understand ourselves and others. We come to realise that we are but a tiny spec within the universe. This can lead us to feel that what we do, who we are, is of no significance. Yet from early infancy we will have become aware of the ongoing interaction that takes place between ourselves and others. Not only is the infant extremely sensitive to the emotional life within mother, conveyed to him in a myriad ways, but he also becomes highly receptive to the responses evoked by his own actions, his physical and emotional communications. I believe human beings have an inborn moral sense, a conscience that even in babyhood can make us concerned at the damage inflicted by greed and destructiveness, in action or phantasy. In contrast, the connectedness of something within and beyond ourselves that is creative, life-enhancing, fills us with wonder. Later in life we may discover a sense of connectedness with the infinite, with what Bion (1970) calls "ultimate reality" which mystics and spiritual people are able to feel in touch with and about which all world religions speak.

I have a picture in my mind of the baby who manages the loss of life within the womb because he is held closely within his parents' caring arms, fed by milk, love, and hope—and is soon able to respond by smiling and making satisfying noises in turn. I see him being able to grow into a child able to struggle with frustrations and disappointments if he is held within his ordinary loving family, encouraged to develop his own resources and to feel that he is contributing to the life of the family. As an adult he may feel himself to be a member of his community and the wider human family, trying to preserve what he has been given and wishing to add to the store of love, knowledge, and beauty which he perceives in some other people and in nature. He may conceive of himself as held within the universe with its rhythm, its cycle of ebb and flow, life, death, and renewal. While feeling infinitely small he may yet be aware that it is within his power to add to or diminish the fund of love, hope, and joy in the world. As our physical strength diminishes towards the end of life, we may come to love and appreciate every small thing that is evidence of the life force within the universe and which will continue beyond our own life-span. Beginning with the intimate relationship to one person, if we have the good fortune to be lovingly understood and go on loving in spite of the frustrations, disappointments, and disasters that are part of life, our relatedness and awareness of connectedness continues to deepen and to extend to ever widening horizons.

What makes such growth possible is the capacity to remain open to and be moved by the wonder of life in what we see and hear and intuitively sense, an awareness of the preciousness of life despite the destructive forces without and within ourselves. It is individuals who are able to face pain and suffering, yet are capable of exuding a spirit of love, who inspire us and make us wish to follow in their path. I remember Tante Rosel, the sister of my grandmother who often came to stay with us when I was a child. She had lost her husband early on in her marriage, brought up her children on her own, and suffered many hardships. She talked about the good things in life and was always in good spirits, busy lending a helping hand. Up at dawn, baking cakes, knitting socks, she was often heard singing: "*Glücklich ist, wer vergisst, was nicht mehr zu ändern ist*" ("Happy the person who forgets that which can no longer be altered"). She did not forget those she had lost but accepted the limitations brought about by her circumstances and was someone who exuded love. We all loved her. I wished I could be like her.

What makes it possible for some individuals to be so appreciative of what life has to offer and capable of bearing suffering? Is it their inborn nature or the way they have been nurtured or a mixture of both? (Music, 2011). Some achieve it through someone's great understanding and loving care, others through experiencing some wonderful event, a spiritual experience that touches the very core of their being. Having once had a glimpse of it, there is the hope of it recurring and this may sustain us through hard times. Such openness to precious moments is not given to everybody. Some minds, hearts, souls remain tortured or closed, like shutters of a camera, unable to perceive not only what is destructive and painful but also what is good, beautiful, life-enhancing. All of us may, at times, have to struggle to hold onto hope, to keep our hearts and minds open and to remain grateful for having been given life—and with it the opportunity to experience the wonders of the world as well as its tragedies.

CHAPTER TWO

From life inside mother to life outside

Most of us have some memories that go back to an experience we had when we were three or four years old; exceptionally, I have met individuals who can remember an event that happened when they were only eighteen months old. Yet psychoanalysis of adults and children, infant observation and longitudinal studies, as well as neuroscientific findings, show that in fact our experiences right from the beginning of life are of crucial importance. They are deeply embedded in our soma and psyche, shaping our physical, emotional, and mental development; they influence the way we relate to others and react to the contingencies life brings with it. Freud stated that nothing is ever lost, that traces of what we have experienced in the past remain in the depths of our mind, in our unconscious. Whenever a relationship or situation in the present in some respect resembles an earlier one, it tends to evoke some of the emotional and physical reactions we had in the past. We experience them in what Klein (1957) called "memories in feelings". Every ending, every beginning, therefore, arouses, to a greater or lesser extent, the physical, emotional, mental states that we experienced at the beginning of our life.

Here is an example of child-like and infantile emotional states experienced by adults at the start of a course—Counselling Aspects

15

in Education—held at the Tavistock Clinic. Having introduced myself and spoken a little about the aim of the course, I suggested that we might be able to learn something from our own experience right now, I invited members to reflect on what they had felt coming into the building, on what it felt like to find themselves amongst a group of strangers and to meet me, the organising tutor of the course. I knew I was taking a risk, that my request might be met by silence but, having assured the teachers that I was not wishing to intrude on their privacy but felt this might be a useful way of discovering what it feels like to begin a new venture, they rose to the challenge. Here are some of their comments: "I feel lost and confused"; "So do I, the receptionist told me where to go but I still twice opened a wrong door; this is such a big and frightening place"; "One feels so alone amongst strangers; I was looking around to see whether there might be someone I know"; "I was relieved when you entered and took control; I felt being in a large group without a leader was frightening"; "I put a cigarette into my mouth to comfort myself"; "I was afraid the person sitting next to me would hear my tummy rumbling as it always does when I am nervous"; "I am afraid I shall find that the way I think about children will turn out to be all wrong"; "I don't know what you are all talking about, I am just excited at being here." The teachers were amazed to discover that as well as having come to the course with very positive expectations, most were feeling considerable anxiety at this first meeting. Getting in touch with their own fears put them in touch with anxieties which continue to exist within all of us, although they stem from infancy and childhood. Reflecting on their own experiences made the members of the course aware of how anxious the children they teach might feel when they begin going to nursery and then start school. It led to a discussion of how little this is usually taken into account and how the transition from home to nursery or school might be handled with greater care.

When I worked as a psychotherapist in a student health service, I saw young people who had been keen and excited at the prospect of going to university but now that they were actually starting student life, panicked at living away from home, feeling lost, unable to manage life on campus and afraid of not being able to live up to the intellectual standard expected of them. The severity of their anxiety was in some cases extreme, leading to fears of having a breakdown or of feeling suicidal. Tragically some students actually committed suicide during their first academic term. To understand the hopes and fears connected with beginnings, we have to go back to the time we were born, the end of living inside the womb and the beginning of living in the world outside.

Being born, leaving mother's body and beginning to live in the outer world, is both an ending and a beginning. The infant is likely to experience it as a "catastrophic change" (Bion, 1962b) which evokes catastrophic anxiety (terror) at being separated from mother's body and coming into this so very different, unfamiliar, outer environment. Such catastrophic fear may beset us when we find ourselves in a foreign country, not knowing the language and unable even to explain where we want to get to. It leaves us feeling totally lost, helpless to find our way back to safety, to known territory.

Bion also put forward the idea (1962a) that the baby is born with a preconception of something that will meet its needs. Are hope and fear based on the foetus' experiences in the womb or are these feelings part of our genetic inheritance? We know from Bion's writing that he conceived the preconception of a need-fulfilling other not only in terms of physical needs but as extending into the emotional, mental, and, I believe, the spiritual sphere. Such a positive preconception enables the newborn to search and feed from mother's breast unless he has had very frightening experiences within the womb; it makes him cry when he is distressed, suffering physical pain and/or emotional distress, in the expectation that his pain will be alleviated by the other. In the course of very many years of studying observations of infants, I have only twice come across babies that did not cry but appeared to keep their distress locked inside them. It seemed that these infants lacked any hope of their cry for help being heard and attended to. Had their hopeful preconception already been affected by experiences in utero?

Here are two examples of traumatic experiences in the prenatal period:

1. Ultra-sound pictures have shown that a foetus, threatened by an attempt to abort it, will curl up and withdraw into a corner of the womb and, just like an animal when terrified of being attacked/ killed, remain immobile, acting as if it was dead. I was reminded of this when I was seeing a seven-year-old child patient who, on meeting me for the first time, stood very still, holding herself stiffly, her back against the door of the consulting room, at times peering at

me anxiously. She was clearly too terrified to move, neither making any attempt to open the door to get out nor to cry. She seemed not to react to my speaking to her about how terrified she was of me. Eventually I decided to see her in the garden where there was more distance between us and this gradually made it possible for her to listen to me and experience me as someone who could understand and verbalise her terror of being in a small room, very frightened of being attacked by me. I learnt later that her mother had unsuccessfully tried to abort her in the fourth month of pregnancy, a fact mother had not told me at our initial meeting.

2. An eighteen-month-old boy was brought by his parents to see the psychoanalyst Piontelli (1992) because they were worried about his extreme restlessness. She observed that the child was looking everywhere in the room as if searching for something he had lost and, at times, was shaking objects as if to make them come alive. When she commented on this, the mother told her that he had been a twin but that his brother had died two weeks prior to her giving birth. Thus Jacob, as Piontelli calls him, had spent two weeks with another foetus whose movements had suddenly ceased. As Piontelli says: "The simple realisation of this, as well as the verbalisation of his fears that each step forward in development, starting from the first warning signs of his imminent birth, might have been accompanied by the death of a loved one for whom he felt himself to be responsible, brought about an almost incredible change in his behaviour" (p. 18).

Ultra-sound pictures have revealed that the foetus is much more active than we used to think. They can even show us something of its characteristic way of behaving which, as Piontelli found, may continue after birth (Piontelli, 1992). The effects on the foetus of the transmissions of mother's varying somatic psychic states have been studied by a number of researchers (Music, 2011). I have found it particularly fascinating to learn that the foetus is able to hear its mother's voice. This already happens, according to Tomatis (1981) and Prechtl (1989), in the fifth month of pregnancy. They discovered that when mother speaks, the motility of the foetus increases; it moves as if enlivened by her voice. We know that babies, once they are born, recognise their mother's voice and are comforted by it, even when she is out of sight. We all know how music deeply affects our emotions; it is responded to even by autistic children. (Hearing appears to be the first of our senses to develop and is, interestingly, also the last one to remain when we are dying.)

It seems to me that the mother's voice adds an altogether new dimension to the foetus' experience—it conveys something of the spirit of what Maiello (1995) calls the "sound object". The voice may convey love, goodness, vitality, and enliven the foetus. Looking at the other extreme, it may convey hatred and be frightening. Maiello gives examples of these contrasting prenatal experiences as they appeared in the dreams of two of her adult patients. One dreamt of dancing to the sound of music in perfect synchrony with a partner, and herself linked the dream to life in the womb. The other patient had parents who were unable to communicate without shouting and screaming at each other. Was it merely the loudness of the sound or was it the destructive quality of their voices, conveyed to this foetus, that led to her refusing, from birth, to accept the breast? It took four years of analytic treatment before this patient was able to have a dream that was not terrifying. Then, for the first time, she reported having had a dream which conveyed a feeling of hope; the extremely primitive content of the dream suggested that it went back to a time prior to being able to hear her parents' voices.

Maiello points out that, unlike the sounds of the maternal organism—the heart-beat, breathing—the sound of the human voice introduces an element of discontinuity in an environment that is otherwise characterised by continuity. She says: "At times the voice speaks, at times it is silent. It is an external object, as unpredictable and uncontrollable as the breast will be after birth. Both the voice and the breast alternate moments of presence and moments of absence"; she goes on to say: "Is it not likely that the disappearance of the enlivening and stimulating voice might give the child a proto-experience of absence and loss? Missing an object generates desire; and desire cannot exist without some, even though fleeting, consciousness of an 'elsewhere' and a 'not-me'" (1995, p. 27).

These ideas stimulated me to ponder the implications of the foetus having a fleeting consciousness of a "not-me", and an "elsewhere". It seems to me that awareness of a "not-me" must arouse curiosity, which we see in babyhood developing into exploration of mother's and father's body; in toddlers, extending to the explorative play with objects; in the young child, in curiosity about mother and father's sexual life, how babies are made and the constant asking "What is this?", "Why?" "How?" An awareness of mother's voice as coming from "elsewhere" makes me wonder whether this might arouse some glimmering notion of a mysterious world beyond the immediate present. This may manifest itself later in life in seeking both scientific and spiritual connectedness with the mysteries of the world beyond our ken, a world beyond our earthly existence.

Being born, the ending of life within mother's body and the beginning of a separate existence in the outside world, is the most dramatic change we are likely to undergo unless we go to another planet—or die. Having lived in a fluid environment where he was automatically fed and held within the warmth and protective layer of the womb, the newborn finds himself in aerial surroundings, exposed to the cold, to the impingement of powerful lights and sounds. Having existed in a confined space with increasingly firm boundaries, he experiences a world that seems boundary-less. With the impact of gravity in the outside world, the ability to move around, which he enjoyed within the amniotic fluid, is also lost, minutes after being born. Unlike most other newborn animals, he is not even able to support his own body weight.

Many midwives nowadays follow procedures that aim to make the dramatic changes the newborn is undergoing less traumatic. These may include dimming the lights, laying the infant on the mother's stomach before the cord is cut, putting him to the breast as soon as possible, thus providing physical in-touchness, immersing him in a warm bath and massaging him, letting him re-experience being in a fluid environment and having a boundary around his skin. All these measures are attempts to provide some sense of continuity for the newborn, similar to what he experienced in utero. Throughout life, something, or someone, who provides a link to the past helps us to bear the loss of what we had before.

The nature of the birth itself will leave its impact. A prolonged labour, especially if the baby gets "stuck" in the birth canal, may lead to claustrophobic anxiety, while my experience of children who are born very quickly is that they are particularly prone to feeling prolonged sadness at having to part from the thing or person to whom they are attached. Post-natal interventions due to prematurity and/or some malfunction, increase the fear of intrusive attacks. There are infants whose passage into life outside is relatively smooth. They use the new capacity of sight to look around with wonder at the new world they have entered. A friend told me that she and her baby spent the first few hours after his birth gazing into each other's eyes. For infants who have had a very disturbed time in utero, coming into the outside world might bring some relief. Yet, they are also likely to carry within them an expectation of the new world being frightening. A mother whose baby son "never stopped crying" for the first few weeks of his life felt this was due to him being so often shaken by the severe fits of vomiting she had suffered throughout her pregnancy.

What is common to all of us is that we come into the outside world in a physically extremely helpless state. The human newborn lacks the mobility to reach the source of food, warmth, and shelter. His helplessness makes him utterly dependent on an other. In the first few weeks, an infant will, when awake, quickly become distressed unless he is firmly enveloped or held in mother's arms, an experience reminiscent of being held within the womb. He will be soothed by being gently rocked, re-evoking the sensation of being rocked by mother's rhythmic gait when he was still inside her; and, most of all, when his tongue and mouth are connected with the breast, the source of food and comfort. The state of blissful security of being held or being connected to mother quickly gives way to screams and frantic movements, indicating his terror when he is in pain or whenever he feels cut off, disconnected from the source of life, feeling dropped, falling endlessly, dying. It is the kind of panic that adults at times experience at the point of going to sleep. Instead of having a feeling of slowly sinking into a safe, containing place, we jump up, startled by a terrifying sensation of falling into an abyss.

Observation of infants shows that even having his clothes taken off may make a baby scream and move in a disjointed manner. As Bick (1968) pointed out, the clothes may be felt as if they are a part of his skin which hold his fragile self together; without the clothes he may feel he is disintegrating, his insides spilling out. He may hold onto mother's eyes or voice but, when feeling not held/unconnected, the young infant tends to resort to what Bick calls survival mechanisms. These may consist of using his eyes as tentacles to hold onto a fixed point on the wall or a light, or alternately holding himself together by the tightening of his muscles, or engaging in ongoing motor activity to maintain feeling alive. While these activities may be helpful as emergency measures to counteract catastrophic anxiety, they may lead to somatic and mental difficulties if they have to be employed a lot of the time. Excessive motor activity may manifest itself in childhood as restlessness, hyperactivity, inability to concentrate. Tightening of the muscles may cause stomach cramps, severe colic, and, later in life, stomach ulcers or hypertension.

Having constantly to defend against terrifying experiences results in the development of what Bick called a "second skin" (thick, like an elephant's), a physical/emotional toughness as a defence against the intrusion of painful sensations and emotions.

More recently, neuroscientific research has shown that satisfying, loving experiences in the first year of life lead to the development of a great multiplicity of neural connections within the brain while the scarcity of good experiences reduces the number of such connections being made and causes brain cells to wither. This evidence confirms yet again that our very early emotional experiences in life are of utmost importance for the baby's development. Although we may not have any conscious memory of our first years of life, the psychosomatic states we experienced then are, throughout life, re-evoked to a greater or lesser extent, in situations that, in one way or another, resemble them. They manifest themselves in our physical, emotional, mental states. Thus, every new situation tends to evoke some of the anxieties we experienced at the traumatic change that took place at the very beginning of our life. Clearly, the more unstructured and alien the new situation we find ourselves in, the further we are removed from what is familiar, the more disorientated and frightened/terrified we are inclined to be. Not only do we feel lost in the unknown situation but we also fear that we are lacking the capacity to manage, that we are helpless as we were in infancy and early childhood. It makes us dread being left without someone to help us.

I have been working with a patient who, when she first came to see me, was terrified at night whenever her husband had to be away on business. She always made sure that a friend came to stay overnight with her; even in day-time she needed to see that there was life going on around her. She had, as a baby and toddler, often been left sitting alone on the beach while her parents wandered off for a while; sometimes they forgot to pick her up. After some years in therapy, she became able to be alone in the house at night but the fear of getting into a state of panic if she were to wake up in the middle of the night, still remained.

Fear of loss in the face of change, of the new, the unknown, extends into our adult life. It may make us cling to whom and what we know, afraid to accept new ideas and to explore new areas of physical/emotional experience. To be exposed to the new may threaten our precariously achieved mental balance, our sense of identity, rules of conduct, and beliefs. It may make us protest and turn against people who expose us to radical new concepts about human life and our planet. That is why Copernicus and Galileo, for example, who changed our concept of the world and our place within it, were persecuted; equally, new findings about the origins of man, like those put forward by Darwin, and Freud's discovery of the unconscious, were for a long time met with extreme hostility and ridicule. Awareness of the prevalence of catastrophic anxiety at any change also throws light on why groups and institutions tend to become more and more conservative and rigidified, unless they are fortunate enough to be inspired by a courageous, innovative leader who is also aware of the emotional/mental threat that any change arouses.

What enables us, what enables the infant, to reach out, go forward and wish to explore the unknown in spite of such fears, is the belief that there is some goodness, something life-giving, life-enriching with which we will be able to connect. Bion (1962a) states that if the preconception of someone who meets our needs finds realisation, that is, is confirmed by actual good experiences, it will crystallise in time into a concept of goodness—a good mother or parts of her in the first instance—which can be reached out to and linked with. Whether the infant's, the child's, preconception is strengthened or undermined is thus dependent on his experiences in the external world.

Psychoanalytic and developmental studies of the relationship between mother and baby have outlined some of the factors that promote mental-emotional development and those that undermine it. A mother who readily attends to the infant's physical and emotional needs, strengthens his trust in a reliable source of help, available when needed. It is of great importance that mother (and father or other caretaker) is able to be receptive to the infant's distress, including the fear of being attacked and dying, can take it in, contain it, and by giving it meaning, modulate it, making it possible for the baby to take it back into himself (Bion, 1962a). Parents will be able to contain their baby's painful emotional states if they are in touch with powerful infantile anxieties within themselves, yet able to maintain a spirit of hopefulness, having faith in their own and the child's life force to combat fear, terror, and despair. Such emotional-spiritual strength conveys to the infant, on a feeling level, that there is something like a mental-emotional space within mother/father/caretaker that allows painful emotional states to be held and contained without going to pieces—that they can be thought about. Through the process of taking in—introjecting—such a holding space, the baby gradually develops a mental space within himself that can tolerate and think about painful feelings. If, on the other hand, he finds his fright, terror, despair, misery are not received, not understood by his caretakers, it leaves him with what Bion (1962b) calls "nameless dread", unspecified, unthinkable thoughts which have continually to be expelled/projected into others. Some mothers/fathers/caretakers may receive the infant's communications but become so terrified that they feed back to the baby their own terror and despair, adding to his own. This is likely to cause him to be wary about what he takes in, physically and emotionally. Might this be one of the causes of anorexia which so many adolescents in Western countries develop? Some depressed mothers allow their infants to invade their body openings physically, using their fingers to bore into their nostrils and ears, being emotionally passive and unavailable. But what the baby needs is for a mother who is an alive presence, as Alvarez (1992) has pointed out.

While the quality of the parents' care is of great importance in helping the infant's physical, mental-emotional development, the child's inborn disposition, his projection of loving and destructive emotions, greatly influences the way he experiences the external world and does so throughout life. Some babies are intolerant of any frustration, react with great anger, screaming, turning away from the mother and take a long time before they are able to be comforted. It may be more than the mother can stand and result in a vicious cycle of a mother getting rough in her handling, speaking angrily, and the baby becoming ever more persecuted. Other babies, born with a less anxious or more loving temperament, quickly recover from distress when mother comforts them. The intimate physical/emotional relationship of mother and baby makes them constantly react to each other in a most intricate way.

We can observe some of the to and fro of losing and regaining a loving connection in the following example: Mark, at eight days, was sucking steadily at mother's breast. When mother removed the nipple from his mouth, he shivered, his hands started fluttering in the air, like a little bird that has lost its hold on the perch and is trying to keep itself airborne. The baby's young, inexperienced mother became frightened by what seemed to her odd behaviour. "He looks mad," she exclaimed and pushed him away from her body. At this, Mark, startled, screamed, his arms flayed about. "He is usually such a good little boy," mother said, almost as if to reassure herself. She held him close and spoke to him soothingly, whereupon the baby calmed down. At fifteen days, when mother in a harsh voice called him "a greedy mouse" because he held on to her nipple for a while after having stopped sucking, his whole body shuddered. Over the next few weeks, Mark's mother continued to feel exhausted, attributing this to the strain of breast-feeding. By the time Mark was four weeks old, he would frequently interrupt his feed and look up searchingly at his mother's face before continuing to suck. When he had finished feeding, he would let go of the nipple and give mother a wide smile. Thereupon she would hug him and shower him with endearments. We can see how sensitive and vulnerable this little boy is to losing touch with the breast and hearing his mother's unusually harsh voice. His subsequent behaviour shows him adapting himself to what mother can tolerate. One might see this as a passive fitting in with mother's wishes prompted by fear, but his facial expression indicates concern for mother. His worry about her makes him behave in a sparing way towards the breast. Yet he is still able to enjoy his feed, appreciative of what mother gives him. His gentle treatment of her reassures mother and his smile of pleasure and gratitude at the end of the feed evokes an outburst of loving feelings from her. We can see how the baby's responses, as well as mother's belief in his goodness, contribute to re-establishing a relationship of love and hope in both of them.

Mark is clearly a very loving baby, very sensitive to his mother's fragility. He may be thought to be unusually so. Yet I have learnt of quite a number of infants who have shown an equal degree of considerateness for their mother's state of mind from very early on. One little girl, at a few weeks old, seemed to sense when her mother was upset and depressed. At such times she became undemanding and indeed tried to cheer her mother up by smiling and making cooing noises. At the other extreme, there are infants who cannot bear to end a feed, show no sign of appreciative pleasure, and cry unless attended to constantly. It is important to distinguish between this being due to a feeling of terror at the loss of connectedness—as the result of a traumatic pregnancy, traumatic birth, or traumatic interventions after birth—or to an anxious disposition, or, alternatively, to the baby's intolerance of any frustration. In the latter case, the baby's terror of being cut off and left to die is added to by the rage which in his mind destroys the source of nourishment and comfort at the instant when it is perceived as not being part of himself. We can observe very similar types of behaviour in children and adults who come for psychotherapeutic treatment. There are those who convey their anxiety and neediness in a way that evokes our maternal/paternal care. They thrive when they find someone who understands them. There are others who are infuriated when their wishes are not immediately fulfilled, have no concept of another person's needs and limitations and whose demanding or destructive behaviour tries our patience. There are also individuals who have experienced severe neglect and so many disappointments early in life that they do not trust or even have a concept of there being anyone reliable, caring, and capable of understanding their suffering. Their fear of being hurt yet again may stop them asking for help. Even when offered help, they may be unable to engage in a trusting relationship and thus become "doubly deprived" as Williams (1997) describes.

Just like the foetus who, though pushed out, also pushes his way into the outside world because the present one has become too restrictive, most of us remain throughout life desirous of extending our understanding, interested in knowing more, widening our experience, connecting with others, finding connectedness with past, present, and future and eventually becoming aware of the interconnectedness of all that has life. Yet there remains in the depth of our mind, the fear of losing what we have become accustomed to, the fear of being as helpless and terrified as we were in infancy. We constantly have to choose: do we dare to risk being open-minded, open-hearted, curious, aware of knowing so little and aware that there is so much to learn and experience? Or do we let the anxiety evoked by change dominate our life? If it is the latter, our mental, emotional, spiritual growth remains limited or, worse still, is arrested.

CHAPTER THREE

Separateness and new connections

In the previous chapter, we looked at the newborn's need for mother to be readily available to make the loss of physical connectedness to her body less traumatic. We considered the catastrophic anxiety aroused when he faces the unknown external environment. This physically helpless human infant with his limited mobility to reach across the space that separates him from what/whom he depends upon has, however, quite remarkable sensory and mental capacities which enable him both to hold on to what offers security and to discover new ways of connecting. He has the gift of sight, making it possible to hold on, with his eyes, to static objects like the wall or light whenever he feels not held by mother's enveloping arms and attention. He uses his eyes to meet mother's gaze, to search her face and her changing expressions which convey her love, her approval, her pleasure, interest in him or, at times, the opposite: anger, disapproval, absentmindedness. At a few months, he will also employ his eyes to keep in contact with mother as she moves about the room. He uses his ears to listen to mother's (and father's) voice and can feel comforted by it, even when she (or he) is out of sight. Maybe the very fact that the human baby is physically unable to reach the one he needs, stimulates him to find other ways of bridging the gap created by separateness. Not only does he use his senses to enable him to do this but he also develops the mental capacity to take in/to internalise and increasingly hold onto good experiences he has had in mother's presence and even, in phantasy, to recreate them.

Mother's ability to feed him, to comfort him, to understand his communications and to relieve his distress puts him in touch with a "thou", different from himself but intimately relating to him. Her beauty and goodness arouse admiration and desire. The emotions she transmits, the sense of security and love she conveys by her presence, arouse curiosity about this mysterious other. This leads him to explore her by looking, touching, grasping at her clothes, making satisfying noises as he feeds, engaging in a mutual giving and receiving.

Meltzer (1988) speaks of the "aesthetic experience" of the baby, overcome with passion by the beauty of his mother. He states that he has never come across a patient, however disturbed, who does not have in the depth of his mind, an image of a beautiful mother. But he also draws attention to how easily this image of a "beautiful mother" tends to be lost. The painful and frustrating experiences the infant undergoes and attributes to mother undermines it, making him suspicious of her. As Meltzer puts it: "He cannot tell whether she is Beatrice or his Belle Dame Sans Merci". He speaks about what he calls the "aesthetic conflict" (p. 22) which arises from the "impact of the outside of the 'beautiful' mother, available to the senses, and the enigmatic inside [of mother] which must be construed by creative imagination". The infant's splitting the image of mother into an ideal and a malign one, which Melanie Klein saw as primary, is held by Meltzer to be a way of escaping from this aesthetic conflict. Infant observation confirms this view. It has shown that some very young infants, as well as feeling alternately blissful and persecuted, depending on alternating satisfying and painful experiences, are also capable of feeling concern for mother. Observations show how much the infant responds from moment to moment to the mother's changing emotional state: her love at one moment, her anger at another; her depression, her inner deadness, anxiety, fragility, her being preoccupied, out of touch with him—all these are sensed and arouse in him, in turn, love, admiration, fear, as well as concern. An adult patient of mine whose mother had always been very anxious and depressed, expressed, in a moving, poetic way, how worried he already felt in babyhood about his effect on mother, saying: "I could not bring the roses to my mother's cheeks." It left him feeling negative about himself and his lovability.

There is indeed, as Meltzer says, much the infant does not, cannot, know about his mother's inside and while much is left to imagination (as one sees later in children's play), I question whether imagination is the *only* way the infant gets to know about her inner world. It seems to me that there is a sixth sense that allows him to be in touch with her internal world, a spiritual connectedness which enables him to sense her love, her faith in life's goodness. This may make her not only outwardly but also inwardly beautiful, an object of wonder and awe. Grier (2006, p. 155) writes: "When an infant is about aged 3 or 4 months old, he or she can be observed from time to time to time to stop … to gaze adoringly into the eyes of the mother (or other primary caretaker). " He says:

> The quality of this gaze is heart-stopping. Although apparently gentle and expressive of deepest love … it is felt to penetrate deep into the very marrow of the mother's soul. The mother feels compelled to respond. But how? [If she can respond by] communicating a love no less profound and searching than that of her baby … this will be, for her, a most profound, deeply satisfying and fulfilling emotional interaction. [It is also] of great significance for the infant's development. He … is learning not only that his love is accepted by the other, but also that that other loves him. Through repeated interactions of this kind, he will, over time, internalise an image of himself as both loving and lovable … building up a core of ontological security.

These are inspiring thoughts. I believe it is within an infant's capacity to sense the reality of something that is in his mother's soul: love, generosity, goodness that fills him with sheer wonder. I conceive the infant's penetrating gaze as trying to fathom the mystery of this goodness with which she is endowed. Not every mother can respond to the baby's loving gaze with profound love, often because she herself has not had the experience of being lovingly mothered when she was a baby. She may feel herself to be undeserving of such adoration and fear that her baby's penetrating gaze will find her wanting in goodness; she may then react by turning away from being looked at, turning away from such intimacy. This is likely to make the infant feel that his love is rejected and discourage him from daring to express, or even from having, such intense feelings of love. In contrast to this, the infant's loving gaze may feed into a narcissistic mother's idealisation of herself, a belief that she and her breasts are of her own making. Showing her breasts off is likely to make the baby feel inferior and to stimulate envy. There are also many mothers who feel gratitude both for having been given a baby capable of such profound love and for having been endowed with a body that can nurture him. They will be intimating to the baby that nature, life itself, is mysteriously wonderful.

It is gratitude, the wonder and awe at the gifts that we are given, which is the hall-mark of a spiritual/religious attitude to life. Great poets and artists speak of being inspired by their muse. Great singers regard their voice as a gift they have been endowed with and feel the need to cherish. Mozart said of the music he wrote that it just came to him as God-given. And we in turn, listening to his and other great composers' music, feel moved and marvel at such God-given gifts. Spiritual healers will tell you that it is not they who have the power to heal but that they are merely a channel, passing on healing energy from some creative source within the universe. Experiences of intense wonder and awe, spiritual in-touchness with something mysterious, profoundly wonderful, are not sustainable for long, not in infancy nor at any time in our lives. They are soon over-taken by mundane, ordinary, everyday emotional ups and downs. Yet these special moments remain as beacons in our lives, sustaining our hope, our belief in the goodness and preciousness of life, a bulwark against suffering and despair in times of stress and misfortune.

Separateness leads from the beginning of life—and throughout life—to the desire to find new ways of connecting. In infancy it results in mother and baby not only responding to one another but engaging in loving intercourse. Mothers and babies imitate each other, coo, smile at each other as well as initiating and developing new patterns of sound and movement. Their very separateness creates a space between them that, as Winnicott (1971) pointed out, becomes a "space for playing" in which the contribution of each partner combines to create something new. Such experiences lay the basis for later creative intercourse with others in play, in work, and in sexual intimacy. They also cause us to have faith in our capacity to be creative in relation to whatever we encounter: constructing objects, playing with ideas, creating works of art, daring to have leaps of imagination which inspire scientific research, and having a sense of connectedness to nature and the world beyond our intellec-tual grasp.

Pleasure in relating to mother who is perceived, in her presence, as separate from the self, feeling loving and loved, is also the first step in developing the capacity to bear separation. For the good experiences are taken in, are stored internally and therefore become capable of being recalled consciously or subconsciously in the other person's absence. In this way the baby can still feel an inner connectedness. He may at first recapture the satisfaction of being fed by making sucking movements or fill the empty hole in his mouth by sucking his thumb; he may recreate the feeling of in-touchness with mother's skin and clothes by rubbing his head against the sheet in his cot or holding onto the blanket; he may recall the sensation of being caressed by stroking his cheek in a similar way to mother. One six-month-old baby was heard lulling himself to sleep by making melodious sounds, reminiscent of mother's singing voice. Dubinsky (2010) speaks of the baby's "musing", playing in a way that is recreating aspects of his relationship to his mother during her temporary absence. Gradually, even without physical enactment, the internal representations of his mother, father, other caregivers and the emotional states of pleasure, support and security connected with these relationships, can be called upon when the child is on his own. This makes it possible for him to have spells of being alone while feeling internally supported, loved, and encouraged. When he is put down to sleep, the baby may at first cry, feel anxious or angry at being left but may increasingly become capable of calling to mind this inner picture of a loving parent providing him with the feeling of being held and comforted, be able to experience the cot as a safe lap-like place, and drift off into a peaceful sleep. Within three months, a baby will be attracted by the aliveness of bright colours, by the movement of mobiles, by the branches of trees waving in the wind as well as by the song of birds. He can thus increasingly bear spells of lying awake, happily engaged with what he sees, hears, and touches.

The ability to internally hold onto a loving connection to the absent person is highly dependent on having received and continuing to receive loving care *and* on the infant's ability to tolerate some frustration. If maternal care has been inadequate, inconsistent, unreliable, unresponsive to the infant's physical and emotional needs, no basic trust can develop. If the infant is so intolerant of frustration that any awareness of mother's separate existence leads not only to temporary anger but to persistent rage, then satisfying experiences are wiped out when she is absent and he will lose hope of anything good surviving. He is then left with an internal mother who deliberately inflicts pain and is persecuting him. Feeling dependent on the person who is felt to have the power to take away this painful state inevitably evokes some fear and resentment. What is crucial is whether this is a temporary state and alleviated by being able to bring to mind the loving aspects of the absent one, thus restoring a good internal connectedness, or whether anger and envy remain dominant. There are children and adults who have had great difficulties to contend with in their early years yet make the best of the good experiences that they have had. I remember Connie whom I met at university. She was brought up in a neighbourhood in which crime was a way of life. Murderousness, violence, drunkenness were all around her. Yet she emerged from this background as an honest, caring person who became a social worker and later fought for justice for the poor, for human rights for all. There are others who hold onto their grudges, neither able to forgive past hurts nor to give prominence to any good aspects of their life either in the past or the present.

The ability to hold onto good experiences develops over the first few months of life. It is not present at the very start of life. There is as yet no thought of past and future: here and now is experienced as the totality of existence. Young infants who have become distressed are often unable to accept the breast or bottle when it is first offered, turn away from mother, experiencing the breast (or bottle) as a bad object. But even at this early stage infants differ, for human beings are born with different temperaments: some quickly regain their good feelings in relation to mother when she comforts them while others take much longer to recover. Winnicott (1949) stresses the importance of the baby being "introduced to the world in small doses", for the reality of separation and the frustration associated with it can only gradually be tolerated. The judgement of how much absence their baby can at any time stand without it doing him harm is often a matter of debate between parents.

Some parents learn from the experience and carefully weigh up what this particular baby can or cannot manage. There are others who hold onto their preconceived views about how to bring up a baby. Some believe they would be "spoiling" their infant if they attended to his distress promptly, that it is good training to let him cry. They may even put the infant out of earshot in order not to be upset by his wailing. At the other extreme, there are parents who continue to be unable to bear their baby's cry for a minute and pick him up at the slightest sign of restlessness. If this continues over time, such children become dependent on someone constantly attending to them and do not develop confidence in being able to cope on their own. The importance of confronting the reality of a parent not being available all the time, provided it is introduced gently and gradually, lies in the fact that absence stimulates the baby to fill the empty space with thoughts and thus encourages the development of mental life and inner resources.

Sooner or later, mother and father will need others to help take care of their baby, at least for some hours. Grandmothers as well as grandfathers are often able to take on that role and do so lovingly. Nannies or child-minders may be employed. What matters is that the baby is given individual, loving attention. This is seldom available in nurseries. Too many babies, children under two, and toddlers are placed for long hours in nurseries where the number and/or training of staff is inadequate to allow for sufficient attention, love, and understanding to be given to each child. Such care is essential for the child's emotional security.

Anxieties and emotional damage to children caused by separation have been thoroughly studied by Anna Freud (1966) and John Bowlby (1969, 1973, 1980). Bowlby also encouraged James Robertson (1952) to film a two-year-old child in hospital. Though it took years for the film to have an impact on policy, it did so eventually and led to hospitals permitting parents to visit their children at any time, even staying with them at night. A subsequent film, showing the devastating effect on a seventeen-month-old child staying in an inadequately staffed nursery while mother was in hospital has, perhaps because it is so upsetting to watch, not had the same influence on policy. It has, however, sharpened the awareness of professionals dealing with mental health problems.

Throughout life, we all struggle with painful feelings when we are separated from those we love and depend upon. Separation can make us feel sad and/or unloved and angry; it may arouse catastrophic anxiety about being left to die, such as we experienced earlier in infancy. Children and adults who have never had consistent loving care and those who have been left too long, too early in life, find separations unbearable. They may avoid entering into a close relationship altogether for fear of risking being left again. One of my adolescent patients was so afraid of being left that she resisted having any feelings about our relationship. For a long time she kept her discourse with me purely on an intellectual level. Even after many months of my always being punctual for our sessions, she always doubted that I would be there at the appointed time. She also stopped talking some minutes before the end of every session so that she could feel that she was leaving me rather than my saying that it was time to stop; every ending felt to her like being suddenly dropped. I found it helped her, to some extent, when I told her a few minutes before the end of the session how much time we had left. Receiving letters from me when she failed to come back after the holiday was of great importance to her. It showed her that I cared and kept her in mind and enabled her to come back for further therapy.

The saying, "Absence makes the heart grow fonder", may be true but only when we feel secure about the relationship. In these circumstances we may become more appreciative of the person we are missing, more aware of how important, how helpful, how enriching their presence is and we welcome them with an affectionate heart when they return. Nowadays, we have the luxury of the telephone, email (and Skype) to keep in touch with the absent person(s) but these connections can break down just when we have reason to be anxious about the welfare of those we love. Telephone and emails are also no substitute for letters which provide a permanent, precious link to the experiences of dear ones we are separated from, including friends and family members who are no longer alive, others we never met, people who lived years and even centuries ago. Letters provide us with knowledge of what happened to them, what they did, thought, whom they encountered, corresponded with, and how they felt in relation to all these experiences. That letter writing has almost become extinct is a great loss both to literature and to our personal relationships. My husband and I used to read the many letters my late eldest sister had sent to my parents and to us, some written more than fifty years earlier. They contained vivid accounts of her experiences, family relationships, the people she met, her feelings and ideas. It put us in close touch with the richness of her personality and a life lived with great intensity.

CHAPTER FOUR

Weaning

From being breast-fed to feeding from bottle, spoon and cup

Being weaned from the breast is a time of painful loss for infants (and for many mothers) except for those who have experienced great difficulties in the breast-feeding relationship. If this has been the case, changing from breast to bottle-feeding may be a relief, allowing for a more relaxed, happier relationship between mother and baby. Some infants are bottle-fed from birth but as long as the infant is held close, it can be almost as intimate a feeding relationship as breast-feeding. Weaning, as used in this chapter, refers to mother cutting down the number of breast feeds she gives to her baby and then ending breast-feeding altogether. The mother's loving understanding of her baby is so particularly important at this stage because the loss of the breast brings with it a revival of the baby's terror of being cut off from the connectedness with mother, the source of life. The infant may be afraid that not only the breast but mother's loving care may also no longer be reliably available. Psychoanalytic work with very young children has taught us that when he is not given the breast, the baby has phantasies of mother keeping the breast to feed herself and/or giving it to father or a baby/babies inside her. His anger, his envy of mother, his jealousy of others who are felt to be getting the feeds may be expressed by biting or hitting the breast, pulling at mother's hair and clothes; in an attempt to possess mother, he may attempt to get inside her by burrowing his head into her chest. When weaned, the baby may, at times, arch his back and turn away from mother either because the closeness to the breast, without being fed by it, is overwhelmingly tantalising or because of his anger at being deprived of it; his sleep pattern may also be disturbed and he may be more fretful and anxious when mother leaves the room.

While some infants are able to transfer the good feelings towards the breast onto the bottle and from the bottle onto the spoon and cup without too much difficulty, most at first protest strongly to these changes. It is in fact a very different experience the baby is faced with: instead of latching onto a warm nipple, he has to get used to a cold, less pliable teat. Being fed with a spoon creates further distance from mother: the spoon comes and goes, there are gaps when his mouth is empty; drinking from a cup makes it more difficult for the baby to control the flow of milk as he could when sucking at the breast or bottle. We may gather from the baby's protesting cry and turning away from these new, alien objects when they are first offered, that they are unwanted. When he is not given the breast, the baby experiences a mother who is not only frustrating in her absence but by her very presence. Some infants react to this by stopping taking the breast from one day to another. Many babies at times hit or bite the breast. Some experience mother's withdrawal of the breast as a punishment for their greed and may fear that they have exhausted mother's supplies and in consequence become miserable.

How mother reacts to the expression of her baby's varying emotions will be crucial in confirming or alleviating the baby's anxieties. She may react by becoming angry, less attentive, though what the baby needs is more attention and caressing to show that she can survive his aggression and still loves him. The baby's aggression and, at times, his misery are hard for a mother to bear at a time when she herself is likely to be in a state of emotional turmoil. In my experience, many mothers are relieved at no longer carrying the burden of being the baby's sole or main source of nourishment and are glad to gain more freedom but they also tend to feel guilty at depriving and upsetting their baby. This may make a mother easily susceptible to feeling accused by the baby's upset and unable to bear his angry attacks. The baby's misery may be even harder to bear. Mother herself may be sad at ending the intimacy and sensual pleasure of breast-feeding and, just like the baby, find it tantalising to be physically so close yet frustrated. When the baby is miserable, she may try to jolly him up by engaging in over-stimulating play. It may be hard for her to let go of this most intimate body-mind interdependency unless she has faith that, although it is the end of a very special relationship, it does open the way to new ways of connecting. If she has trust in the baby's and her own capacity to continue to have a close relationship, she will be able to bear, and help the baby to bear, the loss more readily. The end of feeding from mother's body brings with it a greater awareness of separateness and thus stimulates the baby's thinking, his curiosity about mother and objects in his surroundings as well as his desire to find out what he can do by himself. I am reminded of an eleven-month-old baby whose proud parents brought him to my home to show him to me. It was fascinating to watch this little one crawl around the room, exploring with intense interest the different textures of the floor coverings: lino, wood, carpets; he also investigated the plugs and the holes in the socket they fitted into. I felt I was in the presence of a scientist in the making.

Let us now look at observations of three very different mother-baby relationships and how weaning affected them. The excerpts are taken from observations presented in infant observation seminars.

Ruth is a strong, lively baby who showed her enjoyment of the breast by making satisfying grunting noises throughout her feeds; this gave mother great pleasure. In the first few weeks, Ruth used to go to sleep holding onto the nipple, taking the breast so to speak into her internal dream-world. At four months, she was able to let the nipple go when mother sat her up to burp her. She liked to be held over mother's shoulder, nuzzling into her neck and in this way staying in tactile contact with mother's body. She let out a little cry of protest at the end of the feed but when mother spoke to her, Ruth responded with smiles. At seven months, when mother began to cut down the number of breast-feeds, Ruth impatiently pulled at mother's jumper and when the breast was bared, she sometimes bit it quite hard. "Ouch!" mother exclaimed and withdrew her breast for a moment. "I know you are angry with me but this hurts," she said, and when she had recovered she gently stroked Ruth's cheek, saying "Come on, let's be friends again." In just such ways, a baby learns to distinguish between being somewhat aggressive, as Ruth was at times, and really inflicting pain. Ruth also learnt that mother could be firm, setting boundaries, but at the same time forgiving.

When first offered the bottle, she used to refuse to open her mouth and turn away. When mother widened the hole of the teat so that she could squeeze some drops of milk on the baby's mouth before offering the bottle, Ruth took it more easily. At the beginning of many bottle feeds, however, she spat out the teat, wriggling away from it, showing how disappointing it was for her not to be given the breast. Mother would stroke her cheeks, speak to her gently, and wait for Ruth to calm down before trying to induce her to accept the bottle. When put into her bouncy chair after the feed, Ruth cried in a complaining kind of voice. Mother leant over her, saying "O.K., I'm not putting you back on the breast but I'm still here, I am not going away." Mother's loving, reassuring tone of voice enabled Ruth to stop crying and turn to the toy figure hanging above her head. When put down into her cot in the evening, mother placed Ruth's favourite teddy next to her before she left the room. Ruth's crying sounded at first as if she was cross but then gradually became more mournful as she began to get sleepy.

Shortly after Ruth was fully weaned, mother noticed that when she entered the room in the morning, the baby no longer held up her arms, eager to be picked up, nor did she smile at her but seemed to go on "talking" to teddy. Was she using teddy as a transitional object (Winnicott, 1953) in order to preserve her good feelings for mother, as she had done earlier, or was she now preferring him to mother because she could have him, unlike mother, for as long as she wished? "Are you cross with me?" mother asked. The parents also noticed how subdued the baby had become. "Are you sad, little one?" mother said while caressing her. Mother and father shared their concern about Ruth. They understood that Ruth's behaviour showed that losing the breast made her feel ousted as well as sad and that she in turn was making her mother feel what it was like to be excluded and unwanted. Being able to consider Ruth's behaviour in the context of weaning made sense and enabled them to think about how they could help her. They decided to give Ruth extra attention. Mother engaged her for longer periods in play and conversation, and instead of leaving her to play on her own while mother was busy around the house, she took her with her and talked to her about what she was doing. When father came home from work he not only kissed and cuddled her, as he had always done, but also spoke to her while he had his tea and then took time to play with Ruth before reading the newspaper. In this way the parents tried to show Ruth how much they loved and enjoyed her and that she was an important part of their life. Ruth gradually regained her cheerfulness, and though still needing teddy to comfort her at night, mother and father's company again clearly became of primary importance to her. The parents commented after a while that the baby was now more confident, able to play on her own for quite some time, as well as showing them even more affection than she had done before.

How can we understand Ruth's progress? While at first she reacted to the loss of the breast by projecting her painful feelings into mother, her parents' greater attention and their talking to her while engaged in other activities, showed her how much she was wanted and loved. But when they gave her more attention, she came to realise that her parents loved her but had a separate existence and needs of their own. This led to more deeply appreciating all they had been, and were still, giving to her. It stimulated her to explore the world around her, develop skills, and become more confident in managing, some of the time, to play by herself. All of us, throughout our lives, easily take the good things we have for granted and only come to appreciate them fully when we have to do without them—for instance, our health, our organs functioning as they should.

In Janet's case, weaning was not so satisfactorily dealt with. From early on, her hands took hold of the breast when it was offered and she suckled with total concentration. She protested when mother sat her up to burp her but quickly settled when offered the second breast. She was reluctant to let go of the nipple at the end of the feed, kicked and cried fiercely but soon smiled again when mother cuddled and kissed her. Mother and infant were so engaged with one another, looking into each other's eyes during the feeds that the observer, at times, felt like an intruder into this loving couple's intercourse.

All this changed dramatically when mother, after seven months, began to leave out one breast feed and replace it with a bottle. Janet at first refused the bottle but soon accepted it readily enough. When offered the breast, she would often take a sharp nip at it. This made mother exclaim in pain and scold her: "Naughty girl, don't do that!" Her voice sounded angry and she put the baby down for a while before resuming the feed. When taken off the breast at the end of a feed, Janet no longer responded to mother's caresses as she had done before but arched her back, struggling to get away from her. Mother told the observer that she was very upset by the way Janet was behaving but also very sad at the thought of breast-feeding having to come to an end eventually. She tried to cheer herself up by listening to the radio much of the day. When visited a week later, mother had stopped breast-feeding altogether. She appeared anxious and depressed; the radio was on and so loud that it was difficult to have a conversation. Janet was sitting in her bouncy chair, hugging her teddy bear, alternately talking excitedly to him and burrowing her head in his stomach—just as she had done earlier with mother.

It seems that neither mother nor daughter could bear the pain of losing the intimate breast-feeding relationship. Janet shows by her biting and turning her back on mother how angry she is and deals with her loss of the breast by determinedly turning to an object which, unlike mother, can be possessed and held onto. She avoids mourning the close, affectionate relationship with mother whom she has depended on, loved and enjoyed so much. Some angry behaviour toward the mother, turning away to teddy or some other object, is part of the way many infants react to weaning. But most babies, like Ruth in the example above, can be helped to find their way to re-establishing a loving relationship. Janet, however, seemed unforgiving, did not respond to mother's attempts to comfort her; mother in turn became unable to sustain her efforts to engage the baby and weaned her very abruptly. Janet's bites were no doubt painful but what was far more hurtful was having a baby who no longer adored her. Mother felt so rejected that she was unable to pause and reflect on what had led to the baby's changed behaviour. She withdrew from Janet both physically and emotionally. Perhaps it was her lack of confidence in her mothering ability that caused her to need the baby to make her feel good and loved all the time. Was she unable to experience her baby as a separate individual? Did she identify herself with this idealised baby? Equally we may wonder about the baby's capacity to love her mother when she could no longer fully possess her. Both mother and baby's actions seem to be saying: "If you don't give me what I want, I am so angry, so disappointed, I don't want you any more; I'll not expose myself to being hurt by you again."

The loss of an idealised relationship can become compounded by such hurt that it banishes love and care for the other person. If there is ongoing resentment not only is there a loss of the external relationship but, as Klein pointed out, the loving, internalised relationship is also lost and the person is left feeling empty, lonely, persecuted, frightened or, like Janet, defending against such emotions by manically turning to someone, or something, they can own and control. I hope that mother and Janet will be able to re-establish a close relationship, based not on mutual idealisation as before, but accepting the reality of inevitable limitations, letting go of possessiveness and maintaining faith in each other's loving capacity. But unless this happens soon, there is a strong possibility that this pattern of seeking idealised relationships—which are inevitably bound to fail—will be repeated over and over again. Klein found that the way the early loss at being weaned is managed sets the pattern for how later losses in life will be dealt with.

How true this is was brought home to me early in my training as a child psychotherapist when I was seeing a ten-year-old girl, whom I shall call Marion, for intensive analytic treatment. Her parents had become concerned about her not doing well at school, her inability to maintain friendships, her unhappiness and her fears about death. Her history, as the parents related, was of having been a happy baby, demanding a very great deal of attention. When she was weaned from the breast, she would not accept any food mother offered her; father or her nanny or grandfather had to feed her and the only food she really liked was bananas. I experienced her as a very determined little girl who knew exactly what she wanted. From her many drawings of brides, I gathered that I was to be a fairy godmother who would turn her into a beautiful bride; at other times, I was seen as the prince who had chosen to marry her. None of her problems were mentioned nor did she show any negative feelings towards me. When, after several weeks, I told her that I would be taking a four-week summer holiday, she did not at first believe that I really meant what I said. When eventually the truth sank in, she drew pictures of deserts, of abandoned creatures who had nothing to eat, no shelter to protect them, nothing at all. I spoke about how she felt that this was the state I was leaving her in over the holiday. In session after session she covered sheet after sheet in big letters which read: THIS IS THE END, THIS IS THE END, THIS IS THE END.

After the holiday, it was clear that she had put an end to any good relationship with me. It took many, many months before there was any let-up in her turning her back on me. She sat some distance away from me sucking sweet after sweet, reading, laughing, and totally ignoring me, apparently deaf to my words. She was paying me back in kind for having been so cruel as to leave her abandoned, starved, letting her die. Her behaviour was intended to make me feel what it was like to be excluded, ignored, given no attention while the person you need is having a wonderful time, enjoying herself and constantly filling herself up with sweet, delicious food. I did indeed feel unwanted, rejected, useless, helpless, not listened to, completely ignored and utterly frustrated. It helped me to understand the extent of the pain she had experienced in my absence. I spoke to her about this over and over again and about how unbearable it is to feel like this. I think she eventually understood that my capacity to tolerate such pain without hitting back showed that one can survive it. My containment of her pain and ability to verbalise it for what seemed to be forever, eventually led little by little to some thawing of her icy, triumphant way of treating me. But it took years for her to realise that her anger, her envy, her jealousy, stopped her from being able to make real friends and undermined her ability to learn. Gradually, she began to get on better at school, was able to use her intelligence and make friends.

The following is an example of a baby who, when weaned, underwent a deep and prolonged period of mourning. His very existence was experienced by his parents as a most precious gift, quite especially so as their first baby was still-born. From the beginning, mother and Mathew had a very rich, blissful time together. They seemed to be in touch with one another in a most sensitive, loving way. Mother's handling of him was very gentle yet firm. She sang and spoke to him much of the time, putting into words what she thought he was feeling. When things were painful or unpleasant she would say: "I know this is not nice but we have to do it and it will soon be over." I am sure Mathew did not understand the words but could pick up the meaning from the calming cadences of her voice. When he was four months old, family circumstances forced mother to return to part-time work and thus breast-feeds were limited to when she could be at home. Father took care of the baby while mother was out. Mathew accepted the bottle and fed peacefully, with his eyes closed. I believe that by keeping his eyes firmly shut, he did not have to acknowledge that it was the bottle and father rather than mother who fed him. When father removed the teat at the end of the feed, Mathew appeared upset. When he was put down, he was a little whiny but stopped the moment he was spoken to, picked up, and caressed by father. He was quiet and subdued as father played with him and only became his lively self again when mother returned. Then he was full of smiles, happily accepted the breast and, at the end of the feed, engaged in vocal interchanges with her.

When, two months later, mother had to work longer hours, she was only able to breast-feed Mathew in the morning and the evening.

He steadfastly refused to accept being spoon-fed by either parent. Even at seven months, the only solids he would accept were pieces of bread and butter. He had quite a few teeth by then but did not chew. He kept the bread in his mouth, sucking it until it was soft enough to swallow. He spent much of the time playing with boxes, turning them upside down, checking whether they were empty or full, putting toys into them, and exploring any contents he found in them when he picked them up again. He treated them, like all his toys, with great gentleness. When mother left in the morning, he remained quiet, looking very sad but neither protesting nor crying. When mother returned, he burst into tears and needed much comforting from her before his crying stopped. Mother held him close, chanting and talking to him and when he had calmed down she fed him; they then played happily together or looked at books. Mother talked about the pictures and Mathew turned the pages when mother paused. He treated his toys with the utmost care, though mother encouraged him to be more forceful. She showed him, for instance, how to produce sounds by hitting the xylophone with a little toy hammer but Mathew would only tap the xylophone very gently and so was unable to make it ring out.

We see here a little boy who at first tries to deny the painful reality of the absence of the breast and his mother, literally blinding himself by keeping his eyes closed in order to deny reality and dream of being with mother. He can be comforted by father but when put down, he looks dejected. Once mother is away for most of the day, he becomes a very sad little boy who feels worried that he has emptied the breast. He may also wonder what occupies mother's body and mind when she is away from him, as shown by his preoccupation and gentle exploration of boxes and drawers to see whether they are empty or, alternatively, what is in them. In spite of his frustration and sadness at mother's absence, he holds onto his good feelings for her and is able to relax when he is again in her arms. Only then does he feel safe enough to express his misery, is comforted and becomes able to resume his happy relationship with mother. All this, however, is at the expense of keeping any aggressive feelings at bay. He is so afraid that he will do (or has done) harm that he inhibits the use of his teeth and any forceful activity. When father eventually puts the pieces of bread on the table, instead of holding them out to him, Mathew starts to pick them up and chew them. It would seem that the pieces of bread could now be conceived of as separate objects rather than parts of another person's body. Hands, it seemed, had been equated with breasts which he had tried to protect from being attacked by his teeth. He clearly had, up until then, literally stopped himself from, as the saying goes, "Biting the hand that feeds you". In the same week that he started to chew, Mathew began using his muscles more fully, starting to stand and walk; he also began to play more assertively with his toys. He remained a gentle, very thoughtful and very affectionate child but could now use his strength without fearing that it would damage others. It would seem that previously he had feared that his mother had gone away because he had emptied and exhausted her; perhaps mother's absences were felt by him to show that she was fleeing from this destructive baby Mathew. If such self-accusation and guilt are not overcome, they can lead to ongoing, deep-seated depression and inhibitions which can interfere with the development of physical skills and even the ability to learn. Although remaining somewhat cautious, Mathew became a happy child. By the time he was four years old, he had a great command of language, was curious and eager to learn, spent much of the time looking at books, both with his parents and on his own. He was described by them as being a great thinker. Nor was he easily put off when he did not manage a task; for instance, when making Lego pieces fit and fix together, he would persist until he succeeded. This suggests that he has confidence in being able to creatively restore what is felt to be, or to have come, apart—just like he and his mother, and his mother and father.

 Weaning is a crucial stage of development, putting to the test, like every later loss, the capacity to maintain hope, love, and gratitude in spite of frustration and emotional pain. As Bion said, we constantly make a choice about whether to evade or to face emotional pain. The latter is only possible if there is hope, faith in life beyond the known immediate present source of satisfaction, like the baby (in Chapter Two) who looks deeply, penetratingly into his mother's eyes with a sense of wonder and awe. A baby needs his parents to help him to tolerate the emotional turmoil he is undergoing at being weaned, to demonstrate that they can survive his angry outbursts and rejection and/or his misery, and maintain hope that their love will enable him to bear emotional pain and regain his capacity to enjoy life. Some parents may find it all too much and distance themselves from the infant when he becomes aggressive or may punish him. Some parents cannot stand their infant being miserable, so engage in distracting him or jollying him up rather than acknowledging the loss he has suffered and the appropriateness of his sadness. And yet what is needed is not cheering up or denial of existing emotions but finding, as Ruth and Mathew did, that their pain can be understood, shared, and borne. It is this facing of emotional pain and staying with one's feelings without losing hope which enables all of us at every stage of life to gather strength from being slowly able to overcome the despair at loss. Bion speaks of having faith in "O", the mysterious unknown but sensed "ultimate reality" which is beyond our limited view of human existence.

In fact, weaning brings not only pain at what is lost but also the opportunity for the infant to discover a variety of enjoyable foods. The bottle, spoon, or cup may seem strange and at first be rejected because it is not the desired familiar object but in time the baby can explore the texture, the consistency, the temperature of different foods as well as discover differences in taste and smell. He can learn to feed himself and even play at feeding his mother. At the same time his mental horizon extends as he becomes aware that mother is not the owner of all supplies, that the food she prepares for him stems from sources other than herself. This opens up a whole new perspective beyond the dyad of mother and baby. There is seen to be an interrelatedness and interdependence of mother and father, of the parents and the world outside the family, of human beings and nature. I recall a young mother telling me how her relationship with her ten-month-old baby had entered a new stage after breast-feeding had ceased: being no longer quite so focused on each other, they could now admire and enjoy things together in the outside world—a third object. She described wandering through the garden with the baby on her arm, and the pleasure she derived from showing her the flowers and fruits growing there. As she said: "It is something beautiful which we can share now and later on I hope we will tend the garden together with daddy."

CHAPTER FIVE

Becoming a child in the family

The first birthday of the child is a time of celebration for the family. Many parents feel a sense of relief at having reached this point, happy that their baby—and they—have survived the very anxious, vulnerable time of his infancy. They look back on the year that has passed, amazed at how much their baby has developed physically, emotionally, and mentally, stunned at the skills he has acquired within such a short a time. While aware that he will still need a great amount of attention, they feel freed by his being no longer so totally dependent: he can sit up, move around, help himself to the food put on his high-chair table, and be left for a little while longer to play by himself, as long as he is in a confined space, like his baby-chair, pram, or playpen.

As soon as he can crawl and/or walk, the toddler is able to discover, get hold of, and explore a whole new range of objects. It is a time when parents need to clear away breakable objects which are within his reach. His longer periods of being awake also make him more aware of other people's activities and relationships. All this brings about a new perspective and the need to reorientate himself in relation to this enlarged, more complex picture of the world. Up to now, he has been living much of the time within mother's orbit. Although he now enjoys little forays, he still needs from time to time to check that his mother is nearby.

He seeks physical closeness with her and father to reassure himself of his parents' continuing presence, love, and support. He enjoys looking at pictures, learning to make sounds befitting the objects in the book, or even naming them; he is playing hide-and-seek and being shown how to fit things together and beginning to talk. However much attention, affection, praise, and encouragement he is given at feeding, playtime, bathtime, and bedtime, it may still not feel enough. Mother comes and goes, is often busy. Even when she is present, she does not always focus on him as much as before. He witnesses her paying more attention to father, other adults, other children, even to herself. In all these observed situations, he may feel left out. He longs for the time that he knew himself to be the centre of attention. Some of the time it still seems like this, but it does not last. The loss is profound. It is a time of being weaned from his special position as the baby and having to find his place as a member of the family group.

The transition from babyhood to childhood is an exciting time of discovery but also a difficult one, marked by the arousal of powerful emotions, unfulfilled desires and frustrations. The toddler and young child has to face his jealousy of those mother is with, both when she is at home and when she is out of the house. He enjoys the love and care of father, the games he plays with him. He enjoys the company of older siblings, but awareness of what they and adults can do but he, as yet, is not able to, evokes admiration and envy. He has greater mobility, manual skills, and verbal facility yet finds himself constantly coming up against limitations. How does the young child deal with all this? I am thinking of Freud's beautiful description of his eighteen-month-old grandson (1920). This little boy was observed often playing with a cotton reel which was attached to his chair. The child would repeatedly fling the reel away and then pull it back with an expression of great satisfaction. Each time he accompanied the throwing away of the reel with saying *"fort"* (away, or gone), while every time he succeeded in pulling it back, he would exclaim *"da"* (here). Freud understood this game as the child's way of dealing with his mother's absence by enacting the phantasy of being able to send her away and make her come back again. By symbolically having her on a string, at his command, he could feel himself to be omnipotently in control of mother's coming and going. Put another way, he has not yet fully accepted the painful reality of mother leading a life apart from him, of not being available whenever he wants her. By phantasising being in control of mother, he avoids being angry at her absence as well as the fear of what damage his anger might do to her.

Bion pointed out that throughout life we have to choose whether to face the reality of painful situations, think about them and bear them, or whether to adopt defensive measures designed to evade the pain and, with it, the truth about the reality outside and inside ourselves. He held, as we have seen in an earlier chapter, that the baby's capacity to develop a mind which can gradually learn to bear emotional pain, depended to a large extent on having the experience of his mother (or father or other caretaker) being able to contain his pain, think about its nature, give it meaning, name it. We also have to bear in mind that children, right from birth, differ in their capacity to tolerate frustration and recover from painful situations. Those who have little capacity to do so need adults who have infinite patience and are willing and able to contain the infants' projection of distress, in the hope that with the adults' help they may gradually learn to bear some degree of frustration and pain without ongoing resentment.

The young child's greater mobility makes it possible for him to follow mother around the house; his curiosity drives him to explore every object he can reach, every nook and corner; holes and plugs, so symbolic of the body parts which can be made to fit together, exert special fascination for children. The whole house and what it contains becomes an extension of his interest in mother and father, the contents of their bodies and minds. Yet the young child finds himself being constantly restrained, told "no", "don't touch", "it's hot", "dirty", "dangerous", "it'll break", "spill", "it's too heavy", "it's daddy's", "your sister's", "your brother's", etc. These constraints are unavoidable and it is important to be able to say "no" and set limits but they are a source of constant frustration. No wonder that at times he gets angry and wants to break, throw things, tear papers, grab hold of books and pull them apart—and that one of his first words is likely to be "no". By resisting getting ready to go out when mother is in a hurry, by deliberately throwing food on the floor, he may be asserting his authority and wanting to make the adults feel as helpless about being in control of him as he feels about controlling them. He may also show his frustration by frequent fits of screaming and temper tantrums. His parents may sometimes wish they still had their "good" little baby who could be safely strapped into his seat rather than a child who is so active, so uncontrollable, and looks angelic only when asleep.

Having constantly to protect the child from being a danger to himself and to other people's possessions, dealing with his more forceful aggression, makes it easy to overlook the difficult feelings and anxieties the young child is struggling with. His access to the outer world has extended but this also brings with it greater awareness of what others have, are able to do and he is not yet capable of doing. He may become discouraged and need encouragement as well as a little help to manage what is almost within his capability; for instance, using a spoon, fitting jigsaw pieces together, and dropping differently shaped bricks into correspondingly shaped holes.

Having to face mother's increasing absences, the loss of the special attention he got as a baby, observing the interactions between mother, father, friends, and other children makes this stage of life very difficult. Some toddlers and two-year-old children become very bossy. They bang on the table if food does not arrive immediately they are put in the high-chair, scream if not picked up the moment they ask to be, do not let mother and father out of their sight, throw themselves on the floor at the supermarket while mother is choosing what goods to put into the trolley, grab packets from the shelves and try to open them. It is important to distinguish between the child acting tyrannically, greedily, demanding to have whatever attracts his attention, and such behaviour hiding unmanageable anxiety at feeling that mother is keeping everything for herself, is not interested in him, that he is unwanted, unloved. If his fears are recognised, understood, and spoken about, it may make it a little easier to set limits to his demands and avoid endless battles about who is in control. No longer being the baby who can elicit a lot of attention causes frustration and rage but may alternate with the child being miserable at having to forego the special place he held as the baby in the family.

The youngster's wish to control is linked to both jealousy and envy. He will, from early babyhood, have had phantasies about whom mother is with whenever she is out of sight but her increased, prolonged absences and, on the other hand, his observation of her loving relationships with others—and knowing father and mother are together at night—all arouse increased jealousy. Some toddlers turn with great passion to father, hoping that he will provide what they desire. Marion, for instance, who had always been a very demanding baby, would, once she was weaned, only smile at father, continuing to flirt with him in a coquettish way, and insisting that he should feed her and play with her. When daddy was around, she ignored mother; she was clearly not wanted any more. It was mother who was made to carry the feelings of being excluded, jealous, hungry for attention—feelings that Marion found too much to bear.

The wish to possess one or other of the parents is present in all young children. It is an attempt to re-establish the special two-person closeness they had in babyhood. The child may deal with his jealousy by trying to get between mother and father, to separate them, cause them to quarrel about how to manage him. If he succeeds in doing so, he may temporarily feel triumphant, the "king of the castle", but he will then also be burdened by guilt and fears about destroying their relationship. Oedipal wishes—typically, as described by Freud, the little boy wanting to take father's place with mother, and the little girl wanting to take mother's place with father—reach their height between the ages of three and five. Such desires involve phantasies of eliminating one or other of the parental couple; such destructive, murderous thoughts lead, in turn, to anxieties about a revengeful, punitive father or mother. Frightening phantasies of the witches and monsters that his parents are felt to have turned into threaten to attack him, especially at night-time and lead to nightmares. Driven by jealousy, he may project his own attacking feelings into the parents' relationship with one another and imagine that they are engaged in a hurting, damaging intercourse. All this makes it difficult for him to stay on his own at night. In an attempt to avoid jealousy and the frightening phantasies to which this gives rise he may refuse to go to bed, disturb his parents' evenings, call for them endlessly, and come to their bed at night. It will be important for the parents to consider whether the child is trying to spoil their time together, exploiting their willingness to attend to him, or whether his demanding behaviour is, at times, due to being overwhelmed by anxieties and urgently needing to reassure himself that the parents are alive, unhurt, and still love him. It is difficult for a little child to believe that although he is excluded from his parents' togetherness, he is not forgotten.

If mother becomes pregnant and there is a new baby in the family, the child has in addition to come to terms with the fact that his place as the youngest, the baby in the family has been usurped. It may be felt as an act of betrayal. An adult patient said to me: "Why did my parents want another child, having me should have been enough to satisfy them, was I not good enough?" Wanting to get rid of the new sibling and being more demanding of mother's attention, especially when she is feeding the baby, are all normal reactions. The child may regress, lose some of his previous achievements, for instance, lose urinary and/or bowel control. Alternatively, he may find an important role for himself by becoming mother's helper. Wishing to earn attention and praise may also drive him to try to acquire new skills. He may, at times, identify with the baby's distress and neediness which he so well understands and be kind and gentle to his sibling, taking on a maternal or an older brother role towards the little one. In an attempt to escape the rivalrous feelings towards the baby and the envy of mother's creativity, some children insist that they have a baby in their tummy too and/or that the new baby is really theirs. Others are able to accept the difference between phantasy and reality. For example, when my three-year-old grandson Mossy came to stay the night with me while his father was at the hospital, supporting his wife while she was giving birth to their second child, Mossy cuddled his teddy as he settled down to sleep, telling me: "He is my pretend baby, mummy is having a real one." Being given a pet that the child can cuddle and help to look after, a patch of his own in the garden to grow plants, to water them, witnessing the miracle of seeds growing into stems, buds opening into flowers, becomes an important source of feeling capable of caring, being creative, and playing a part in nature's creative process.

By the age of three or thereabouts, the child is far more able to handle objects and understand their function, and his ability to verbalise has much increased. Most children's curiosity at this age is boundless. They are likely to ply their parents with endless questions: "What is it?", "How does it work?", "Why, why, why?" The scientist, the philosopher, the engineer is developing, seeking to understand nature, mechanics, cause and effect in his external and internal world. He may even come to realise that when he has been nasty and has hurt someone, he feels bad inside. Equally, he may discover that when he is kind and loving or trying to make amends, he feels good.

A whole new vista of creative possibilities and interconnections opens up before the child's eyes. For a time he may think that his parents are all-knowing, all-powerful, but sooner or later he discovers that they too have limitations, do not have answers to all of his questions, nor can they protect him, themselves, or others from being subject to pain and illness, cannot prevent pets and people dying. He loses his utter reliance on omnipotent parents to solve his problems. This, however, may drive him to find out things by himself, to experiment, use his creative imagination in play and making objects, wonder and speculate about his immediate environment and the world beyond his ken. Children love being told stories. I still remember the ongoing stories of the naughty little boy Noe-Noe which my father told us at bedtime. His name derived from the fact that he always answered "No-no" whenever he was asked to do something and the stories were accounts of the scrapes this got him into.

The freshness of the child's experience of life, his appreciation of beauty, his lively imagination, and the way he applies the information he has been given, become a source of enrichment, joy, and amusement for others, as well as for himself. I remember Mark, an autistic three-year-old child, one day discovering the beauty of the coloured windows on the landing in my house. He stood, fascinated, with a beatific expression on his face, gently repeating: "Lovely, lovely roses." I also recall how amused we were when our Raphael, aged four, staying with his grandparents in a hotel in Scotland, announced one day that he had met God. Asked by the adults "Where?", "How?", he said: "It's the porter, he sees everything, he hears everything, he knows everybody and what they are doing!"

The first five years of life are the most formative. We have already looked at the ways in which the foundations of physical, mental, emotional development are laid down in babyhood but this continues into the first years of life and the role parents and other carers play in providing an interesting, stimulating, enriching environment at home and in the outside world, is important. While the child is born with his unique endowment, the way his character develops seems to me to be greatly influenced by his immediate and extended family during these precious early childhood years. Struggles between possessiveness and sharing, between dependence and independence, ignorance and knowledge; acknowledging differences in age, experience, sexual organs; relationships with others within and without the home: all begin to take shape at this time of life. The child will be greatly helped by parents who answer his questions honestly, understand his struggles, and are tolerant. But it is also important to be able to set limits, to say "No" (Phillips, 1999), "This is enough", when the child behaves destructively; it helps him to know there are boundaries and it is in fact less frightening than being allowed to do whatever he wishes. I remember Dr. Esther Bick telling us, her students, about a girl of five who was smashing not only toys but crockery, flower vases, anything breakable. One fine day she cut up mother's favourite hat; yet mother neither did nor said anything to stop her. The little girl shouted: "Don't you care about anything?", showing her dismay that nothing, including her need to be helped to stop being destructive and feeling guilty, had received attention. Escalation of destructiveness in childhood and adolescence is frequently a hidden plea for help.

The time of young childhood is a period of transition from which the child emerges with a greater awareness of his own identity, his place within the family, of himself as one amongst a multitude of other people. He learns the importance of love and care for others from his parents' example—or, alternatively, selfishness, hatred, and hopelessness. He becomes aware of other living creatures, of animals, whose fascinating antics he can watch at the zoo; he enjoys pets that he can cuddle, feed, play with; he notices the beauty and scent of flowers, of plants in the home, the garden, and the park; the texture of soil, of sand, the variety of shells on the beach—all these exciting discoveries fill him with joy and wonder. Awareness of the riches of nature may be nurtured—or limited—by his parents' love of—or lack of appreciation of—life in all its varied forms.

CHAPTER SIX

Going to nursery

In many Western countries some children are sent to a nursery when they are still babies. The length of maternity leave varies from country to country. It may be a few weeks or a few months (Sweden is an exception, allowing both mothers and fathers extended leave). A baby, a toddler, a child under the age of two and a half years needs a reliable person who gives him individual attention and responds to his communications with understanding. It is rare to find a nursery that has enough staff to meet this need. While mother is working, the individual attention the little one needs can often be given by a grandmother, grandfather, or aunt; alternatively, parents who can afford paid help might engage a good nanny or child-minder.

Going to nursery, provided the child is not too young, can help a child to learn to share and make friends with children of his own age and acquire new skills as well as enjoy group activities. But even at the age of three, starting to go to nursery, being separated from mother and home, even for a few hours two or three times a week, presents the child with a very major change. He may at times, accompanied by his mother, have visited mother's friends and their children. When he knew them well, he may have been left there for an hour or so but coming to nursery faces him with a multiplicity of new experiences, all happening at

become very independent. She was keen to go to the nursery that her older sister was attending. There is a close relationship between the staff of this small nursery and the parents of the children. Lucy and her mother were encouraged to visit the nursery for an hour a week for several weeks before Lucy started to attend on her own. When she joined the nursery, she had no difficulty in parting from mother but was at first very tired by the end of the morning and more than usually demanding of mother's attention at home. She appeared a little anxious when her mother went out; at other times she was defiant and bad-tempered. Lucy was well prepared and the transition to nursery had been gently and thoughtfully handled; the disturbance at beginning nursery was minimal. But, as we can see, even in these circumstances a child is likely to feel some degree of anxiety and anger. As her very experienced nursery teacher said: "You never know how a child is going to react. I always insist that mother stays until I feel the child is ready to be left. It may take anything between one and six weeks. If mothers have to go out to attend to other matters, I need to have their phone number so that I can ask them to come back if the child becomes upset."

How difficult any particular child finds it to manage the transition to nursery depends on a number of different factors:

1. The child's inner equipment, that is, the inner security he has developed on the basis of reliable, understanding parenting.
2. How different the new experience is from what he has experienced before.
3. The way beginnings and endings have been managed in the child's past.
4. The way the beginning of going to nursery is dealt with.

Going to nursery provides a crucial step in the child's development, helping him to become a little less dependent on mother. Provided that the nursery is well staffed and has a nurturing, warm, happy atmosphere, it will soon become a place where the child feels at home, enjoys many interesting, stimulating new activities, and makes friends.

This is how the head of a nursery summarised her goals for the children in her care: "To learn to become an active member of a group; to have their voice heard; to take initiatives within that group; assert themselves when necessary and sustain cooperative interaction with others around them. To be able to withdraw from the group and at times play on their own, concentrating on what they are working on."

Ending his time at nursery in order to start going to school, having to part from all the attachments the child has made at nursery, is likely to be painful. The ending needs to be prepared for well beforehand so that there is a chance for both the anger and the sadness that the loss evokes to be worked through. As the end becomes imminent, some children may, because of their jealousy of the younger children taking their place, have sudden outbursts of tearing paintings, breaking toys, or becoming aggressive to their teachers. Some teachers feel hurt and rejected by such children. It helps them to tolerate such behaviour if they are made aware that the children may be passing on to them (projecting into them) the feelings they find too painful to bear: feeling ousted, rejected, envying the exciting times the new little children will enjoy, missing what they have come to love. If teachers can tolerate the destructive and rejecting behaviour of the children and continue to care, the child's love and sadness will in most cases come to the fore. As one little girl told her mother when she was about to leave the nursery: "I love my green room, my dear room, I will miss it." Teachers also often find it hard to part from the children they have become attached to. One teacher reported that she had recently become very short-tempered with the little boy who had been her favourite. She had told him that he was only producing rubbishy pictures. In the process of recounting this to the psychotherapist who was acting as a consultant to the staff, she said she was really going to miss this boy and suddenly realised that rubbishing his work had been her way of escaping from the pain of losing him.

Such attachment to the children may also make it hard for nursery staff to prepare children for the transition to school. On the other hand, some nursery teachers, realising the difficulties children will encounter in the change from the familiar and protective ambience of the nursery to much bigger groups and a far larger building, contact the school the child will be going to. They may even take the child to see the classroom they will be in and talk about the child with their future teacher and head teacher. Such bridge-building is very helpful, showing the child that he is held in mind both by the old teacher and by the new one. Such nursery teachers show by their example that it is possible to care beyond the ending of seeing each other, that there is a continuity of love, linking past and future. If endings can be dealt with in this way, there is an external loss but the past good experience can be internally retained, enabling the child to enter into a new phase of life with greater confidence.

CHAPTER SEVEN

Beginnings and endings in school

Beginning to go to junior school

Many children entering primary school will have been attending nursery and thus have some experience of leaving home for part of the day, being in a group, and relating to staff. All the same, beginning to go to school faces all children with a very new situation. In a good nursery, children will have been given some individual attention and learning will have been acquired through a mixture of work and play. At school, all learning takes place within groups; attention needs to be paid to the teacher, standing in front, presenting knowledge in a much more formal way. The group the child finds himself in is much larger than those he has been used to hitherto. At break-time and mealtimes he finds himself one amongst a crowd of children, most of them older and bigger than himself. Indeed, everything is on a much bigger scale: the building, the play area, the number of classrooms, corridors, toilets. Although most schools offer an introductory day where the newcomers are shown around, there is so much to take in that a lot of the information given will not be absorbed and the child is likely to feel confused and lost in these new surroundings for quite a while. While the child may be excited and impressed by the pictures and the writings of pupils displayed on the walls, evidence of other children's achievements may arouse too great an expectation about what he should soon be able to do and may also cause worry at how much will be expected of him.

In Germany, where I started to go to school, it was the custom for parents to give the child a huge cone-shaped container full of sweets on the morning of his first day at school. Was this a present to celebrate this exciting event or a consolation prize to sweeten the frightening step into a more grown-up world? Probably both. Family and friends of the family tend to congratulate the child on being big enough now to go to school and while this might make him feel proud, the child may be worried that he is no longer permitted to have baby-like and young-child-like fears. On his first day at school five-year-old Luke announced: "I am a big, brave boy now, my little brother is just a silly little baby, he cries when mummy leaves him." Not only must he not cry but feelings of loss, confusion, fear were treated by him with contempt, as being silly, babyish, and he laughed at those who were anxious. His own pretence at being so grown up soon broke down, leading to a refusal to go to school. He was only able to return after a number of psychotherapy sessions in which his fears could be admitted, worked at, and accepted as a part of himself.

Some schools make special arrangements to allow children to settle in. They accept only half the group in the first term and the rest three months later. Children who have been there longer are then encouraged to look after the newcomers. Children may at first be allowed to come for a few hours only, increasing to a full day's attendance once they are happy to do so. Such schools tend to employ teachers who are sensitive to the children's vulnerability and aware of how important it is that the teacher knows the child's name and thus his/her identity. Five-year-old Lily at first made sure every morning that mother had attached her name label to her blouse. After two weeks she announced that she did not need it any more: "My teacher calls me by name, she knows who I am and whom I belong to." To be remembered by the teacher makes the child feel that he/she is not lost in space. Crises centring on feeling lost and abandoned can, if handled with understanding, be very temporary, as in the following example. Cathy, who had been very confident at nursery, became very clingy shortly before she was due to start school. During the first weeks at school she would sometimes suddenly start crying, unable to be comforted. Her thoughtful teacher asked an assistant teacher to fetch Cathy's older sister from another class. Having her sister next to her, just for a few minutes, was enough to make Cathy feel that she was not abandoned, that her sister was nearby and within call. After her sister left, the teacher kept Cathy sitting close to her. Soon she did not need this special attention and was given a star for "bravery". This she showed off proudly to family and friends, saying that she now liked school.

By no means all problems are that easily dealt with. The transition to school, like every new situation, presents a change which may bring to the fore deep-seated problems, less evident until then. David, for instance, had always found it difficult to separate from mother but within the very protected environment of a small nursery, away from home for only a few hours, his anxieties had been manageable. Being at junior school, one amongst a large group of children for many more hours, brought to light the weak foundations on which his sense of self was built. The teacher referred him for an assessment because of his extreme restlessness, his inability to listen and concentrate. When I saw David, it became clear that he hardly heard what the teacher was saying because his mind was totally occupied with thinking about home and wanting to be with his mother. He felt lost and frightened and his hyperactivity was a way of holding himself together. He was afraid of literally coming apart, his insides spilling out. He told me that he did not like writing because "I am afraid of all the pooh coming out." Such infantile fears showed an inability to symbolise (Segal, 1957); the ink was, in his mind, concretely felt to be the same as "pooh" in his bottom. He certainly needed psychotherapy.

Going to senior school

Parents and teachers are often surprised to find that the move from junior to senior school can be a very disturbing experience. Even choosing the school is a fraught issue, requiring a lot of thought before deciding what kind of school is suitable for a particular child. Some children, for instance, need a very structured setting while others flourish in a freer environment. The academic record of the school tends to be given paramount importance by many parents while the need for encouraging imagination, creativity, and development of individual strengths is often given little consideration. Whatever the parents' views, it is important that the child's preferences are listened to. The decision about which school to apply for is followed by a period of uncertainty about whether the child will get a place at that school. There is great disappointment when the chosen school does not have a place for the child or when the child does not do as well as others in the exam and interview and is not accepted. To obtain a place in the preferred school is a great relief and a cause for joy. At the same time, it may also make the child anxious about whether he can live up to what he feels is expected of him at this "wonderful" school.

The move from junior to senior school involves quite a dramatic change. Buildings tend to be vast, the number of children maybe in the hundreds or even thousands. The child will find himself one of the little ones among pupils so much taller and stronger than he and this might be frightening.

The headmaster of a senior school who was attending the Tavistock Clinic's course for teachers, told me that he regularly puts aside some time during the first two weeks of the academic year for the eleven-year-old new boys to talk about how they feel about coming to his school. He was astounded to discover how free they felt to talk to him, once they were encouraged to do so. Most of them said they would not tell their mother or father—although some told the grandparents—how they felt about the new school; hardly any dared tell their older brothers or sisters for fear of being laughed at. Most chose pets; as one boy put it: "I whispered it all into my cat's ears." And what is the sort of thing you can only confide to pets? Matters like: "I was terrified of the teacher and especially of the headmaster. I thought I might be examined, cut open like in an operation and that all the mess inside would be seen"; "I was frightened of the other boys, I thought they might be bullies"; "In my dream last night, there was a whole crowd shooting at me"; "I am afraid I'll be failed, be found not to be good enough for this school" (Salzberger-Wittenberg, Williams & Osborne, 1983).

The change to senior school may bring to the fore a problem which has been more or less successfully defended against up to this point, as in the following case.

Six months after joining the senior school Freddy was one day so overcome by panic that he rushed out of the classroom and ran all the way home. Ever since, he had refused to go to school and a home tutor was eventually provided. He had no learning difficulties and after a while he managed to see his home tutor on the school premises, provided his mother accompanied him there and he did not have to join the other children. Some months later the school counsellor referred

Freddy to a child guidance clinic because the boy had threatened his mother with a golf club. Freddy told the therapist that he had been extremely furious with his mother because she had allowed his younger sister her own choice of a television programme while he had wanted to watch a football match. He was a keen and good football player but had dropped out of his team because he feared the other children's taunting of him. He told the therapist that he had enjoyed junior school and spoke of how much he wished he could go back to a place where he was the big one and could tell the younger ones what to do. What had frightened him at senior school were the big boys who bumped into him as they ran down the stairs while he was fighting to make his way upstairs to the next lesson. What emerged during his first meeting with his therapist was Freddy's inordinate rage with mother for giving in to his sister's wishes and ignoring what he wanted. He had previously enjoyed being the boss in relation to her and the younger children in junior school, keeping them from challenging his position. All this suggests that he had never come to terms with his anger with mother for giving birth to his sister, letting her have her turn at being nursed at the breast and getting more attention than he because he was older. He had taken on the role of a nasty older brother who dominated her and kept her in a lowly position. Being at senior school, therefore, not only faced him with being small in comparison to the big lads but left him feeling threatened by the older ones who were experienced as wanting to boss him, humiliate him, and prevent him from coming up to their level of development, strength, and achievement, perhaps even wanting to kill him. Such paranoid fears only lessened when he, with the help of his therapist, became able to begin to take responsibility for his own murderously jealous feelings instead of projecting them onto the older boys at school.

It is possible to provide a modicum of security for newcomers to the school by appointing older boys and girls as guides to the young entrants; also by keeping the newcomers together in the same group and place, thus providing a holding framework until there is some sense of familiarity with the new environment. Usually, the opposite is the case: it is common practice in senior schools (in the United Kingdom) for teachers to stay in their room, thus forcing pupils to take themselves and their belongings to another classroom at the end of each lesson. All this adds to feelings of being lost, confused, uncontained, in bits, lacking a sense of identity. Frequently pupils are assigned to different groups according to their academic ability in different subjects. Grading of pupils may be useful in some respects but it may mean being with different boys and girls for different subjects, making it harder to make friends and feel part of a specific group. Break-times may be fun but also expose the child to being pushed around in a crowd, mixing with some children who are almost twice his size. The need to feel strong rather than afraid may make it tempting to join a gang. Other children who don't join may live in fear of bullies. Often, too little supervision is provided, especially in breaks and when the children arrive and leave the school grounds. And all this lack of containment and protection occurs at a time when boys and girls are undergoing great physical changes and all the emotional upheaval puberty brings with it, including confusion about their identity.

Competition about academic achievement and sport is often given far more emphasis than character development. There are other schools, however, which consider that the aim of education is to help the whole person. Such schools stress kindness and consideration for other people, respect for children from different backgrounds, different nationalities, different religions. They lay on exchanges between children from different countries. They may involve the children in taking care of the school gardens and teach them about climate change. Youngsters in the sixth form are also often expected to undertake some voluntary work, perhaps visiting or helping old or disabled people.

Endings at school

In many schools, children have a new form teacher each year. Depending on the relationship the child has with the teacher, having a different teacher may be met with disappointment or be welcomed. It is mainly the unexpected changes which evoke considerable anxiety: staff turnover, sickness, changes in the designation of tasks means that the class may temporarily or permanently lose the teacher it has come to know and rely upon. The powerful feelings which such changes arouse are usually disregarded. This is in large measure due to teachers underestimating the important role they fulfil for the children and the group. They are therefore usually unaware of the anxieties that can be stirred up by any change. A class that has had a number of different form teachers in quick succession may undergo serious disturbance. As members of one such group put it: "No one stays with us, they don't seem to like us and it's just not worth making the effort to work hard anymore."

That even a temporary transfer to another teacher can provoke powerful reactions was brought home to me when I asked a group of adult students to reflect on how they felt about my having asked a colleague to take over from me for the next three weeks (Salzberger-Wittenberg, Williams & Osborne, 1983). Here are some of the thoughts they expressed: "Oh dear, we'll have to start right from the beginning again and go back to all that chaos." "It will be strange for you not to be here, we've got used to you now and that feels safe." "You hold the memory of the group." "When you go away the link gets broken." These comments show that an important part of the teacher's function is to provide a safe framework within which learning can take place, for learning requires being open to something new, as yet unknown, and to all the anxieties this arouses. The teacher is felt to contain the group as well as the helpless, frightened aspects of some of the members within it. Without the teacher's containing presence the group and the individuals within it may be afraid of falling apart, losing the link to their more capable selves and past good experiences. Such anxieties evoke infantile anger with the person who causes this situation, as expressed in remarks like the following, expressed by my teachers' group: "You are deserting us." "You don't care about us, you just pick us up and put us down." Or more triumphant remarks, disparaging me for leaving them, like: "You made us work hard, it will be nice to have a rest." "I expect the new teacher will be better, more interesting." These comments were followed by the teachers giving voice to their phantasies regarding the reason for my absence: "You have been looking tired, perhaps you are not feeling well and need a rest." "Maybe you are fed up with us, can't stand us anymore.""Perhaps you prefer another group."

Teachers are usually not aware of the impact that their absence, even for a short time, may have on their pupils. It is not enough to casually mention that one is going to be away for a while. Space has to be given in which feelings of anger and worry can be vented before and after there has been a disruption. If a teacher leaves his job permanently, it needs months of preparation, yet most teachers wait until the last moment to tell the class, sometimes because they feel guilty at abandoning their group. Few teachers allow the pupils to express their feelings. They are often surprised and hurt when pupils become hostile or turn away from them. Enough time needs to be allowed so that it is seen that the teacher survives the onslaught of aggression and denigration she is receiving from her pupils. If this is understood by the teacher as being due to the children's feeling of loss, she will be more able to tolerate such feelings and be able to continue to be interested and concerned about her pupils. This gives children the chance to compare phantasies of a weak, rejecting, or punitive teacher to the reality of a teacher who goes on being friendly and caring. In such circumstances, it becomes possible to part on good terms and retain a more realistic and often appreciative memory of the relationship.

School holidays

Holidays provide the opportunity for rest, relief from hard work, the chance to engage in activities not available at school, a time to be with one's family and friends. They may indeed be looked forward to with excitement, especially by those whose families offer positive alternatives to school life. But the end of term is also often fraught with anxiety, anger, and depression. It is significant that vacations are generally referred to as "breaks". What is it that is broken? Is it the link to the group and/or to the teacher and the function he fulfils for his class? By the nature of his role and/or personality, he may be experienced as being like a good parent, providing knowledge and care, holding each pupil in mind and carrying the hope for the child's development. The teacher's absence threatens to break this security, bringing with it the fear of being forgotten or dropped out of mind. On moving to another classroom at the end of the school year, children want to ensure that they leave their mark in the room they have been in, stick pictures they have painted onto the wall, scratch their names into desks or write them into books with indelible ink. Some, unable to bear being left, take ending into their own hands, finding some excuse to stay away from school during the last few weeks or days of the term. Others, resentful at feeling left, show their jealousy of whoever the teacher is felt to be with by literally breaking parts of the school's equipment, even smashing furniture or smearing the walls with graffiti. It is a way of saying: "If we can't have you, then we will not let anyone else have anything of value from you either."

Holidays from school involve the loss of being a member of a group. One is no longer part of a unit. Not only is there an actual separation from members of one's group but children's expectations of what the holiday promises may differ considerably. There are those who can look forward to being at home, visiting members of the extended family, having time with friends, going away to interesting places, having fun.

Other kids may not have many or any of these opportunities; they sit at home, lonely and bored. And there are those whose families are fragmented, unstable, financially and/or emotionally impoverished. These children cannot help but feel envious of those who are more fortunate. As a twelve-year-old who was in therapy with me said: "Everybody is asking me where I am going on holiday; well I'm not going anywhere; my mother is working all the time and we can't afford to go away. They ask what I am going to do with my dad but I haven't got one. They ask what presents I am getting for Christmas and I don't want to tell them it isn't going to be anything special. I feel like screaming and kicking those who are so lucky to have so much more than I have."

During a long break when the whole of the teaching staff and student-body go away it can feel as if the totality of the fabric of what one has relied upon has gone. The closed school building, empty and without life, may evoke fears of the place having been destroyed, being dead. Moreover, the absence of the firm structure of the school day, with its timetables, set tasks, and rules, has gone. Breaks throw children back onto their own resources. They give them the chance to use their imagination, to use the time creatively. On the other hand, some may feel at a loss. The freedom that holidays provide exposes them to experiencing an emptiness or chaos within their internal and their external world. Some children become so depressed that they wander around the streets aimlessly or, in order to enliven the dullness of the days, and envious of what others have, engage in delinquent acts. Some turn to drugs or alcohol.

Difficulties in settling back to work after the break are often related to resentment at having been left by the teacher. It is important for the teacher to show that she has kept the pupils in mind, for example, by showing that she remembers what occurred prior to the holiday. This can help to gather the group in and create an atmosphere of togetherness in which learning can again proceed.

Leaving school

Many adolescents yearn to leave school, to be free of the demands and restrictions it has imposed on them. They want to taste freedom from the structure of school life, to be part of the adult world, to be active rather than sit and study all day long. While this is part of a healthy wish to enter a new stage of life, it may also be used as an escape from inner difficulties, indicating a belief that these can be left behind. Moreover, an over-emphasis on all the benefits of ending school tends to ignore the anxieties connected with ending a time of relative security and now having to take on new responsibilities. Worries about the future are often either denied or hidden from others. Teachers have an important role in helping students and their parents make realistic plans based on their knowledge of the students' abilities and shortcomings. I am reminded of the story a headmistress reported to me. When she told the mother of one of her rather poorly endowed pupils: "I am afraid he is not going to be a high-flyer" (a great achiever), his mother commented: "Oh, never mind, he doesn't like flying." Pupils who have done poorly may be anxious about exams or about the demands that will be made on them by an employer or by further education. They may absent themselves from school because they are depressed and tell themselves that if they have not yet learnt enough, it is too late to do so now that their school days are coming to an end. Others deal with their lack of progress by denying any difficulties in themselves, believing that it is the school that is holding them back from having a more satisfying life. Yet quite a few of these same adolescents tend to come back to their former teacher, seeking reassurance and comfort from him once they have had a taste of the much greater demands made on them in the world of work. Even those who are doing well at school and are given evidence of their achievements when they get the results of their exams, may still have doubts about how ready they are for what lies ahead. Those hoping to go to university may not only fear the competition they will have to face but also the responsibility they will have to take for their studies and an independent life. In as far as they have relied on the structure provided by the school, such as set homework and the attention of their teachers to maintain their interest in a subject, they will find it hard to continue learning when left without such supervision.

Endings of school life tend to be blurred. Pupils who leave before they have reached the final year tend to drift away without their leaving being acknowledged or any event taking place to mark the occasion. For those who complete their time at school, there is an emphasis on preparing the youngsters for the final exams rather than widening their horizons. In the last few months, much of the preparation for examinations takes place at home with only the occasional visit to school. Exam results come out after schooling has ended and therefore there is often no opportunity to discuss the results with teachers and be supported by them, especially when the results are disappointing. It would seem that after all the hard work which has gone before, the school timetable is organised in a way which ensures that stressful feelings prior and post exam time, thoughts about what has and has not been achieved, and what it means to part after many years of being together, are all avoided. Often there is no leaving event, no rite of passage and no proper saying good-bye from the staff group. Pupils are simply left to say their good-byes to friends and walk away, feeling that their leaving is of no significance to the teachers and the headmaster/headmistress. One wonders what is being avoided. Is it too painful for the staff to say good-bye to their students? Are the students envied for being young and having exciting opportunities in the outside world while teachers stay to carry on with their demanding jobs? Is it too painful for staff to meet with pupils who have failed or not done as well as expected and face the pupils' and their own disappointment? Do teachers want to evade their students' anxiety, and their own, about whether they have been prepared well enough to go out into the big, wide world? Does saying good-bye to another group of youngsters make teachers aware of the passage of time, of getting older, feeling left behind, sad, bereft of the pupils they have come to like and are attached to? Do they therefore prefer to concentrate on the new intake of students they expect next year rather than paying attention to those who are leaving?

Most teachers care deeply about their groups, miss pupils they have become especially fond of and those whom they have helped through difficult times, witnessed their growth, taken pleasure in their achievements. And yet what teachers and students feel about each other is not given space to be expressed and worked through: neither the anger at failure nor the resentments are faced but remain as unfinished business. But neither are gratitude, acknowledgment of good experiences they shared, nor sadness at parting addressed. Seeing that the teachers do not speak about how they feel about the relationship coming to an end, students tend to assume that their teachers don't care that much about them. What a sad situation, what a missed opportunity to learn that it is possible to part in a good, appreciative way.

CHAPTER EIGHT

Tertiary education and entering the world of work

Tertiary education

As well as excitement, feelings of insecurity are experienced, to some extent, by all students when starting life at university. This is hardly surprising when we consider the great changes in lifestyle which are involved: from a structured school timetable, set homework, close supervision to mainly unstructured studies and unstructured days; from being part of a group of girls and boys of various grades of ability to finding oneself amongst a peer group of extremely bright, highly achieving youngsters. Having had a family to fall back on, the young person is left without adults looking after his welfare; having been part of ordinary life, he finds himself floating in a rarefied atmosphere. Having done well enough academically to be offered a place, he may feel that he is expected to be brilliant or at least to have to prove that he deserves to be amongst the elect. In contrast to the fixed curriculum at school, especially in the last two years in order to achieve good exam results, the intellectual freedom to play with ideas at university, while immensely stimulating and liberating, may be experienced as being uprooted from a firm basis of orientation and lead to mental/emotional giddiness and confusion. Even for the more secure, the more mature, amongst the students, the changes involved are great while for others they may be all too much. The latter may be amongst those picked up by staff working in a student health or counselling service. But by no means all who are deeply unhappy or at risk of breakdown have the courage to seek help. Many are too ashamed to do so or even to admit to themselves that they need help—after all, one is supposed to be a grown-up! So the young person tries to act being adult, pretends to be fine, sometimes at great cost to himself. Parents may feel inhibited about keeping in close contact, afraid to be thought to be intruding into their youngster's life. Yet students are financially dependent on their parents and contact with the family is needed to keep the young person grounded. Most university staff, because of the false assumption that all that young people want is freedom from adult authority—falsely conceived of as authoritarian, oppressive, and interfering—leave students to fend for themselves rather than considering the students' welfare and making themselves available to be turned to when needed. As a result, many students feel very lonely, lost, and uncared for and have to rely for support exclusively on members of their peer group. They may be lucky enough to find congenial friends but others, in order to avoid loneliness, are easily drawn into less helpful groups. Some may try to escape painful feelings by turning to drink or drugs or seek comfort by sleeping with another lost soul, of either sex, like babes in the wood. Some break down and have to return home, some commit suicide or attempt to do so.

Here is an example of a student in his first term at university. The student health doctor was called in when Mr. A. was found by his landlady in a comatose state. When the young man told the doctor that he had drunk himself into a stupor because he had become extremely depressed, it was suggested that he might like to have a few consultations with the therapist on the staff. Mr. A. agreed and was sent an appointment to see me a few days later. He arrived forty minutes late, staggered into my room and sank into the chair opposite mine. I wondered whether he was drugged. When I asked him to tell me why he had come nearly at the end of the hour I had reserved for him, he said that he had only just woken up after taking an overdose of sleeping pills. I offered the interpretation that he seemed to want to show me how desperately he needed to be taken care of but I did not on this occasion enquire further about his suicidal gesture. I said instead that I would like his doctor to see him right away and that we would talk further next week. Mr. A. was subsequently sent to the local hospital for a stomach wash-out and was kept in for a few days.

When he came to see me the following week, he told me he had been quite happy in hospital and very glad that his mother had come to visit him. When I asked him to tell me what had led to his taking an overdose, he replied that he did not really know, he had never done such a thing before. He had been feeling very lonely and depressed, and then drank a whole bottle of wine. When he woke up he felt even more depressed, had another bout of drinking, and then took the pills. I commented on his loneliness and his inability to stand the pain of depression which led him to try to drown it or even try to put himself to sleep forever in order to escape such feelings. Mr. A. said he had only been drinking heavily since coming to university six weeks ago. He explained that he had not made any friends and felt very lonely in his digs but then added that he had actually been depressed on and off for as long as he could remember. This led me to ask him about his family. He said he came from a large family; this was because his mother adored babies. It was "heaven" to be a baby, you got all you wanted, were cuddled and carried about all the time but when the next one came along you were dropped, mother gave all of her attention to the new baby and you were left to fight for yourself. I commented that perhaps coming to university seemed to have felt to a child part of himself as if he had been thrown out of a protective home and his mother's enveloping care, in the same way as he had felt dropped and abandoned by her when a new baby was born. It seemed that taking an overdose on the eve of coming to see me was a communication to me that was something like: I shall die unless you take me into your maternal care. I think his being kept in hospital for a few days was also more a response to his emotional than his medical need; he certainly managed to evoke in everyone the feeling that he needed to be taken care of.

It seems that Mr. A. had never come to terms with the losses in early childhood. Leaving home and finding himself in a new environment stirred up feelings of loss and insecurity of a catastrophic nature while being amongst peer group members brought back unworked through jealousy of his siblings. Let us listen to how Mr. A. experienced being a newcomer: "I felt completely lost on the big campus; one is a nobody, travelling around in a vast space, in an endlessly changing succession of groups to which one does not really feel one belongs. No one cares whether you are alive or dead. They would not even know you were dead." When I asked him why he had not contacted his tutor to tell him about how awful he felt, he said: "I know I could have gone to see him but he has not given any indication of being interested in me as a person, all he cares about is that I do well academically. I also did not feel I could go and tell him that I was miserable, failing to manage on my own." We can see that the tutor was equated with a mother, in his mind, who was felt to have no concern and no empathy for the vulnerable, child part of him. His tutor, like his mother, was only felt to be interested in having him grow up quickly and manage on his own.

In subsequent sessions, we explored his deep-seated infantile feelings of anger towards his mother, still demanding to be taken care of as in babyhood and experiencing the lack of such special care as total abandonment. I pointed out to him that his internal picture of an uncaring mother did not seem to match his external mother who had in fact kept in touch with him and came immediately upon learning that he had been admitted to hospital. It also became clear that in choosing to stay in private accommodation rather than on campus, he had hoped that the landlady might take on a mothering role. We then spoke about his difficulty in making friends because others in the group were felt to be rivals for attention, like his siblings. Towards the end of our three sessions, I told him that I would like to see him for a follow-up appointment at the beginning of next term but that he could contact me earlier if he again felt desperate.

When I saw him next, we jointly decided that it would be better for him to move into a hall of residence where there was a warden in charge and where there were others students with whom to share daily domestic tasks. The work we did enabled Mr. A. to continue with his studies and begin to join in social events. He was aware that help was available if needed and I suggested that it might be important to get further help to deal with his rivalry with other students.

Coming to university offers rich opportunities for acquiring knowledge, making friends and contacts, sometimes for life, having fun as well as being intellectually and emotionally challenged. It is at one and the same time exciting and disturbing, posing a threat to the individual's sense of identity. This arises in the first place from the loss of the familiar environment, having to look after oneself in an atmosphere of great competitiveness. How all this will be dealt with depends to a large extent on the inner strengths the individual has developed on the basis of previous experiences and also on the extent of the external change involved. Hence, feelings of strangeness and loss will be particularly acutely experienced by those who have never lived away from home, students who have come from abroad, from a different culture, and have difficulties with the language. It would seem that parents and the staff of universities are often ignorant of the feelings of loss and the catastrophic anxiety some students are prone to experience when they enter this new kind of life. They therefore do not provide containment at this point of major transition. In recent years, many young people have chosen to have a "gap-year" between leaving school and going to university. This provides a useful transitional period in which to have work experience, to travel, and to learn to become a more self-reliant and responsible adult.

As well as the loss of the familiar external world, we need to bear in mind the disturbance in the internal world of the student caused by encountering such a wealth of knowledge, ideas, and inspiration. Being open to new ideas, looking at things from a different perspective, involves letting go of some assumptions and beliefs that have up to this point informed his mind and sustained his mental equilibrium. Taking on board new ideas, while perhaps exciting, changes the picture we have of the world, both as it was in the past and is in the present; it may feel as if one's world is turned upside down. Can we bear to open our minds or is it too frightening to do so? Do we feel humiliated by being so ignorant and unimportant in this big world of knowledge, of learning? Bion called the state of mind that is unreceptive to acquiring knowledge and pursuing the truth "-K", while he called the state of mind that searches for understanding and truth "K". This latter state requires the ability to bear uncertainty and sustain the fear of helplessness in the face of the unknown, unthought of until now. An imaginative leap into the dark, and a wait for insight and understanding, is needed for the discovery of truth; as Keats says: "Being capable of being in uncertainties, Mysteries, doubts without any irritable reaching after fact and reason" (1817).

For some students the intellectual brilliance of their professors and some of their peer group may stir up the kind of idealisation and envy felt in early childhood towards parents who were held to be the possessors of all knowledge and inner riches. This brings to mind a student who was referred to me by her doctor because no physical cause could be found for her frequent attacks of vomiting and diarrhoea. When asked when these attacks occurred, she told me that they happened when she sat in the auditorium, listening to lectures; also when she was reading in the library. In the session with me, she constantly interrupted and corrected me. For instance when I said: "You seem worried", she said: "No, not worried—anxious." When I, in the next sentence, said: "You seem to be anxious", she said: "No, not anxious—worried." She continued to correct the words I used and I soon found myself stumbling over every word and becoming almost unable to utter a proper sentence. It was a very disturbing experience. When I paused to think about what was happening, it occurred to me that she was attacking what I was saying, turning it into fragmented bits, like vomit and diarrhoea. I pointed out to her that she seemed to have lost sight of the fact that our meeting was meant to be a co-operative effort to understand the symptoms she was suffering from. "A co-operative effort," she exclaimed. "I always experience a relationship as one being at the top and the other at the bottom. It is the same with my boyfriend." This made it clear to me that anyone who had something which she did not possess—a penis or knowledge like the lecturers, me as a therapist and the authors of the scientific books she was surrounded by in the library—made her feel that they had "it" and that she was just a bottom. This caused her to be enraged and to attack what the other person was felt to possess. Such a state of mind is typical of someone dominated by envy. I do not know enough about her early life to decide whether she was born with a particularly envious disposition that spoilt everything she did not own or whether her mother who had the top (breast, milk) had shown herself off in a narcissistic way, making her baby feel humiliated—just a bottom—and hence provoking envy.

The idealisation of academic knowledge which is so prevalent in centres of higher education tends to stimulate ambition and competitiveness. This may lead some students to become identified with a highly idealised, intellectual group whose hallmarks are feelings of superiority and contempt for others into whom the unwanted, needy, helpless, ignorant parts of themselves are projected. However, when examinations loom on the horizon, worries about not having done enough work, fears of being examined about what one has really learnt and of not doing well in exams, questions about whether one is equipped to enter the world of work without the guidance of one's teachers at one's side, all force themselves on the student's mind. This is the time when many come to see a doctor at the student health service with somatic problems.

Mr. M., a third year political science student who was referred to me because he had been complaining of severe headaches and soreness in his eyes, told me that when he had been writing recently—emphasising that he had written a number of important articles—his head sometimes felt so tense, so tight, that he thought it would burst. At night, he had difficulty in getting to sleep because ideas about all sorts of projects that would bring about useful changes in society were racing around in his head. He began telling me of a number of ideas he was developing and spoke so quickly and unremittingly that my head was becoming full to bursting point. I voiced how I was feeling and added that it must be hard to go off to sleep when your head is bursting with ideas. He said that he could not relax and often woke up in the night haunted by thoughts about the future. Asked when his symptoms had started to trouble him, he replied that it was when he thought about his studies coming to an end and about beginning to prepare for exams.

I asked Mr. M. what he was planning to do after he had finished studying. He thought he would probably have to go back home to Africa unless he did so well in his exams that he was offered a postgraduate fellowship. He reported that his tutor thought very highly of him and expected him to get a first-class degree. His tutor had intimated to Mr. M. that he was one of the best students he had ever taught. I said that I gained the impression that as well as feeling driven to work harder and harder, he was also trying to run away from some painful thoughts and feelings which might come to his mind when he thought about his future. I had noticed that he seemed reluctant to entertain the idea of going back home. Mr. M. fell silent and then told me that shortly before he had left home and come to England, his father had had a stroke which had incapacitated him. He used to own a grocery store. I learnt that the family had never been well off and now lived in very straitened circumstances. There were six younger siblings and mother was struggling to look after them. She had become very depressed after the death of one of the children, killed in a road accident. Mr. M. said he saw himself as having to provide financial support for the family. If he were to go back to Africa, he expected to get a high government post.

After a pause, he then added, rather quietly, that he was really hoping to stay in England. I suggested that perhaps he was investing so much hope in this because it would be hard to go home to the sad situation he had described and have to support his family, not only financially but also emotionally. Maybe, he might even be expected to take on the role of being the head of the family. At this tears welled up in his eyes. He told me that he had not been home for three and a half years. It was so expensive and it had taken him a long time to get used to the climate here—and, as an afterthought he added "and all that". I wondered what "all that" might be. He said that he had felt very strange when he first arrived in England, he had felt so out of place, so unimportant amongst all these clever and well-spoken people but then he had learnt to fit in, to sound and behave like the others. He had tried to model himself on his tutor and had worked extra hard to please him. But he was afraid that he might not do as well as expected and that would mean disappointing everyone and, he added after a pause, "I suppose, it would mean going home."

We began together to understand the enormous strain he was under. His head was full to bursting point because he felt driven to be this wonderful "head" boy, to be either an academic or else somewhere near the head of government in his home country in order to get away from feelings of helplessness in the face of the depressing situation that awaited him there. His own desire to be in a powerful position had been promoted by his family's wish for him to be different—"not be spat on by others"—and through his achievements to pull them out of their lowly state. His own and his family's ambitions had been abetted by his tutor's praise. All these pressures had resulted in Mr. M. catapulting himself to heights he now feared he might not be able to live up to, for they had, it seemed, not been achieved by steady growth but by pro-jectively identifying himself with his tutor and the English university establishment who were seen as omnisciently clever and omnipotently powerful. He had cut himself off from his roots, from his family and his emotional connectedness to them because it was all too painful to think about. It seemed he had not mourned his father's loss of capacities nor the death of his brother. He had now reached a point of crisis where his head was full of ideas, ideal aims that had been erected as a barrier against the knowledge about the poverty, the disasters and misery that were awaiting him at home. His outlook had become hardened and his eyes were sore with unshed tears. When we began to speak more about his family, his mania gave way to feelings of guilt and depression and some reparative wish to show more concern for those he had left behind. The wish to stay on at university seemed to be an escape from intimate, caring relationships and a drive to attain status through accu-mulating degrees and publications.

There are, of course, others who decide to pursue an academic career because they are deeply interested in developing their ideas in greater depth and imparting what they are discovering to promising, gifted students. In 1947, Pandit Nehru defined the objectives of a university in this way:

> It stands for humanism, for tolerance, for reason, for progress, for the adventure of ideas and for the search for truth. It stands for the onward march of the human race towards ever higher objectives. If the universities discharge their duties adequately, then it is well for the nation and the people.

Such ideals, I believe, would still be subscribed to by many who govern and teach at universities, although by no means all live up to them. What is rarely recognised is that few students are able to attain the capacity to search for the truth—and bear it—as well as to be tolerant and caring about human relationships without the support of an understanding family and/or a caring educational environment. As two of the cases I have described show, this support is particularly important at the beginning and ending of life at university.

Looking back at my time as a student, I realise how extremely fortunate I was. Not only did I enjoy the knowledge and intellectual stimulation which the university provided but I lived in a community of Quakers who were exemplary in exercising tolerance and concern for others whatever their age, nationality, or faith. The building we lived in was simple and was surrounded by a large, beautiful garden with a lake at the bottom of the sloping lawn which provided a space for peaceful contemplation or serious one-to-one discussion. We had a lot of fun as well. At the end of every term there was an evening of making music, reading poetry, putting on shows that made fun of members of staff as well as of ourselves.

Entering the world of work

Leaving university, using the knowledge acquired and putting it into practice at work, requires another major change of lifestyle and different skills. Coming back to life outside may mean facing a reality that is disappointing. The ideals which inspire many young people to want to bring about a better world need to be harnessed to an awareness of not being omnipotent, learning to consider the complexity of the external world and of human beings and the difficulties of bringing about change. Reality so often interferes with idealism and vision. Even a man like the United States' President Obama who, after many years of successful work, was elected on the platform of promising to bring about change, is an example of someone of great integrity, idealism, and liberalism who nevertheless failed—apart from having persuaded Congress to legislate for a universal health system—to implement the changes to bring about the fairer society he had hoped for. He has been unable to deal with strong opposition and unforeseen obstacles.

Many young people who enter employment are disappointed at having to start at the bottom and work their way up at a slow pace. Having every bit of his work closely supervised/inspected makes the new employee feel treated like a baby, incapable of doing anything on his own. The world of work may be more demanding, tougher than he had expected. He will have to keep to fixed times, often working long hours, at the beck and call of senior staff and managers. Nor is one necessarily protected from disappointment if one remains within the academic world. Not long after getting a diploma (with distinction) in social sciences, I accepted my professor's invitation to come back as a lecturer. I did so on condition that I would be allowed to take the extra subjects needed to obtain a degree (the diploma course had meanwhile been turned into a degree course). Having had such a happy experience as a student, I returned to university with high expectations and indeed it felt good not only to be teaching but also to study at the same time. I was called "baby don", partly because of this peculiar situation and also because my age and my efforts were treated with tolerance. I was appalled, however, to discover the cut-throat competitiveness which can exist among academics. Many seemed to want to show how clever and superior they were by engaging in destructive criticism, picking holes in their colleagues' lectures and publications. I soon realised that I did not want to remain in academia but needed to learn a lot more about human relationships and follow my long cherished desire to be actively involved in what tends to be referred to as a "caring profession". I found a note in my diary, written when I was eleven years old that read: "I want to learn to help people to help themselves [presumably to have a better life]"—not far off the mark of ending up, as an adult, studying social sciences, doing some social work, and then training as, and becoming, a psychoanalytic psychotherapist for the rest of my working life.

Studying at university has until recently been considered a time to further one's general education as well as to pursue subjects of one's choice at greater depth. (I say until recently because choosing which subject or subjects to study is, in the present economic climate, often decided on economic grounds, on what will offer a greater chance of finding a job afterwards.) Many students, especially those in the humanities are at a loss to know what they want to do once they obtain their degree or degrees. They require help to discover what they really care about, what kind of work will make their life meaningful and satisfying before they embark on an additional training for a particular occupation or profession. Those taking a degree in one of the sciences or in engineering are more likely to know what kind of job they are looking for. This also applies to those who study medicine, social work, or nursing; they will, in fact, already be doing some practical work during their years at university. Such students/trainees are prone to being overwhelmed by the pain, distress, frailty, poor living conditions of their patients/clients and need someone to support and contain the anxieties aroused in them in order to avoid distancing themselves emotionally from those they are trying to help. Otherwise, their wish to be reparative can easily degenerate into referring to patients as "the gastric ulcer case" or "the kidney failure one" or "the child abuse case", indicating how unbearable distress can be evaded by turning a blind eye to suffering and turning human beings into mere scientifically interesting objects. The need for emotional support and containment for students/trainees, in order to avoid adopting such an uncaring attitude as a defence against emotional pain, usually remains unrecognised and is consequently either not provided for at all or is offered but insufficiently.

Many young people try a number of jobs before deciding what career to pursue. Work can bring great ongoing satisfactions once one has got established: feeling wanted, needed, being valued for what one achieves; finding the work interesting and meeting interesting people; learning to be competent, confirming one's capabilities and discovering a speciality within the field of work which leads to further development. Earning his living makes a young person feel proud, it makes him feel that, at last, he is an adult; it is a relief to no longer be totally dependent on parents and/or the state. Most importantly, it can lead to having a sense of making a contribution to the lives of others, to one's community, to society. It also raises the hope of being able to have the finances one day to get married and support a family of one's own.

In the present circumstances, all this is very difficult to achieve. The economic crisis in Europe, the United States, and many other countries has led to wide-spread unemployment. There are hundreds of applicants for every job advertised. If they are lucky, graduates may eventually find a part-time or temporary job; only very few will be offered a permanent position. In order to earn some money, graduates may accept doing menial work on an ongoing basis, such as stacking shelves in supermarkets, which blunts their minds; they live in limbo while their applications for jobs are rejected again and again. Feeling unwanted, useless, is soul-destroying. It is hard not to succumb to depression, hopelessness, despair. Many just give up trying to find employment and simply live on unemployment benefits and roam the streets. No wonder that juvenile delinquency, alcoholism, drug addiction, all kinds of mental health problems, are on the increase. While a stable home environment may help to keep up the young person's morale, it is likely to feel uncomfortable for the youngster to have to live at home again for an indefinite period, dependent on his parents. Being forced back into an adolescent position undermines the natural development appropriate at this stage in the life-cycle. It often creates friction between the parents and the youngster. Some students returning home may find that father and/or mother are also depressed and angry, having been made redundant and struggling financially. One cannot help feeling worried and sorry at the state of the world so many young people are inheriting. What seems to be required nowadays is to have a great capacity to tolerate living with uncertainty, to show entrepreneurship, use ingenuity to create work for oneself and set up one's own business.

There are also quite a number of mature students, for instance, men who have served in the army or women who wish to re-enter the world of work after bringing up children. They may have felt confident in what they were doing before and developed firm attitudes and convictions. They may find it difficult to unlearn some of these and to have to start all over again in a world that has changed so drastically.

CHAPTER NINE

Getting married

Phantasies about being married already arise in childhood. Freud's discovery of the Oedipus complex—that is the wish of little boys to take father's place with mother, the girl wanting to take mother's place with daddy and the resulting anxieties arising from the rivalry with the parent of the same sex—is well known. These phantasies are based on the desire to own the parent of the opposite sex, body and mind, and to be *the* loved one. As Klein has shown, they have their roots in the infant's desire to possess mother totally.

In childhood we learn from fairy-tales of a girl who turns into the most beautiful of all women and is chosen by the prince; and of a boy becoming the cleverest, most daring man whose deeds earn him the right to be given the princess in marriage. The stories end, either by implication or explicitly, with "and they lived happily ever after." Some children continue to live in such a phantasy world, as did my patient Marion who, when she started psychoanalytic treatment at the age of ten, made it quite clear to me that I was to be the fairy godmother who had the magic to make her into a most beautiful bride. At other times I was the prince who adored her and would never leave her. More commonly, children of that age have a more realistic idea of marriage, although they may, at times, dream of a fairy-tale kind of relationship.

I well remember the long discussions with my sister night after night—she might have been eleven and I eight years old—about the kind of homes and family we would one day have. It was worked out in great detail, although the looks and qualities of our husbands remained rather vague. We were quite sure about the kind of house we each would have, the number of rooms, the size of the garden which, of course, had to have a swing in it; the number of children we would like to have, how many girls and boys—it was a large number—and the clothes we would dress them in, the food we would cook for them, and the games we would all play together in the garden before breakfast. I don't remember our phantasies extending much beyond the early morning! Such wishful thinking was only to a limited extent based on the experience within our family although faith in a loving couple and their love of children was no doubt influenced by the example set by our parents.

In adolescence, sentimental, romantic films and novels easily induce teenagers to identify themselves with the beautiful, sexually attractive men and women portrayed. It is often an escape from feeling unattractive, lonely, unloved, and inadequate. Such fears may lead to seducing or being seduced into sleeping with any boy or girl who shows an interest in them. Becoming a fan of a sexy singer, a sportsman, a film star whose portrait adorns the walls of the bedroom, is a widespread adolescent phenomenon.

In adulthood, marriage beckons to provide love, happiness, and companionship. The choice of a partner and whether to get married to him or her is probably *the* most crucial decision we have to take in our life. It is, after all, meant to be "until death do us part". Being in love is often considered to be inevitably suffused with idealisation, making one blind to the beloved's faults, shortcomings, and any negative aspects of his or her character. That may frequently be the case but there are many couples, equally in love, who before deciding to get married, try to allow time to get to know each other, to discover each other's likes and dislikes, what they find irritating about the other, and attempt to honestly discuss and argue about their different views and whether these are acceptable or at least can be tolerated. What seems to me to be of the utmost importance is to find out what each partner values, what ideals they wish to try to live up to, what path in life their heart, their spirit, seeks. The relationship may then not be based on idealisation but on the conviction that one has found a soulmate one loves and feels loved by. It brings with it a heightened intensity of experiencing the world, an awareness of the beauty and preciousness of life in all its manifold forms. As one young man told me: "I have always loved being out in nature but since I have found Helen my experience of it is so much richer: the grass is greener, the blossom more beautiful, more delicate, the trees exude more energy"—an echo of the passionate love of the infant-mother relationship? The love of the partner may extend to wonder and awe at the bounty of life, of the whole of creation. It sets the lover and the beloved alight. It is this that makes me, to this day, fascinated and enlivened when I look at the glow and beauty of two people who are deeply in love.

Getting engaged marks the decision to be committed to each other, a feeling of responsibility for the partner; a desire to get to know this unique other more deeply and, in most cases, a wish to have children. Once the intention to get married is made public, what emotional upheavals might the young couple and their families go through? In the weeks following the public announcement of their engagement, as congratulations from family and friends pour in, the couple are likely to be carried along by the pleasure, the excitement, the hope that their forthcoming marriage evokes in others as well as in themselves. To have found someone who loves and cherishes you may be felt to be a matter of luck, magical, undeserved, amazing, wonderful. To feel able to commit oneself to another person and to take on the responsibility of caring for the other throughout life, is rightly felt to be an achievement. The couple's parents may also be glowing with pride—provided they like the person their son or daughter has chosen. Their offspring's readiness to enter into the state of marriage is felt as a confirmation of their having parented him/her well enough to enable this step to be taken. There may also be some relief at being able to hand over the care of their child to another person, for however old their son or their daughter may be, he or she will, up to this point, have been considered by them to have been, ultimately, their responsibility. Concern for the child lasts a lifetime.

Thoughts about how their lives will change loom large, not only in the couple's minds but in the minds of the couple's families. In the first place, the parents of the couple will want to know: has their daughter/ their son made a good choice, will she/he be happy, cared for, and provided for? Will they gain another son/daughter or lose contact with their child? Brothers and sisters also wonder how the couple will, in future, relate to them. I am thinking of a boy of twelve, Dave, and the very close relationship he had with his much older brother who had always given him a great deal of attention and affection. Now that his brother spent so much time with his fiancée and was seldom available, Dave went through a very painful time of feeling unwanted, excluded and worried about whether, once he was married, there would be any place for him in his brother's life. Indeed the whole extended family—cousins, aunts, uncles, grandparents—are affected by the prospect of the young couple's marriage, for what is at stake is the closeness or alienation, the harmony or disharmony, of family relationships as well as a concern about whether family values and traditions will be passed on to future generations or be replaced by totally alien and/or unwelcome ones. One thing is certain: the nature of the relationships will change. It is for the couple to decide where and how they want to live. Members of the family will have, at least to some extent, let go of the important role they may up to now have held.

"Love is a desire of the whole being to be united to something, or some being, felt necessary to its completeness," says Coleridge (1811–12). The other's difference is in fact what completes the self and therefore the other has to be allowed freedom to be himself or herself. It means being aware of the other's needs, the wish to protect, take care of, bring joy to the beloved, his/her happiness enriching her/his own. Yet admiration and love may be spoilt by envy of what the other has—whether it be beauty, talent, success in work or social life. Any of these may arouse the desire to possess what the other enjoys; or to own rather than value the person who has these desired assets. Greed, envy, jealousy, possessiveness, competition, interfere with love of the other to whom one is linked, with whom one is at times united but who remains separate from the self. And with such recognition of separateness, other aspects of past relationships come to the fore: can the other be trusted, will they accept me as I am or demand that I be what they wish me to be, will they turn against me if I have different needs? Can I be allowed to be angry, will disagreements lead to withdrawal of love? It is important to test whether the partner can take one's aggression, whether the relationship is strong enough to withstand conflict.

As the date of the wedding draws near, it is not unusual for the young couple to panic about whether they have made the right decision. Their doubts tend to centre both on their own and the other's shortcomings as well as how they will relate to each other through all the ups and downs of life. Will I find the other one's habits, moods, jokes, complaints, tastes, mannerisms intolerable? Do we have enough interests in common? Will we get bored with one another? Will I really be cared for? Will I be supported in pursuing what is important to me? Will I be criticised, restricted in my freedom, undermined, be the one who always has to give in, do what he wants? Will I have any time to myself, any privacy? Can I live up to his expectations? Does he really know me? Will he put up with me when he finds out what I am really like? Some of the ruminations are based on the pattern felt to have governed the parental relationship, such as: I don't want to be a domestic slave like my mother. Will he leave me, be unfaithful like my dad? Will she be like my mother, always feeling superior because her family is richer, more classy than mine? Or: I want to be as admired as my mother was, will I be? I want to be as caring and responsible as my father—will I be able to be like him? Such questions often make the engagement period a most uncertain, stressful time. Frequently, there are last minute considerations as to whether to break off the relationship before it is too late. It will be hard to communicate the depth of such anxieties and doubts to people one is close to without feeling disloyal to one's partner or fearing that one will be judged to be too immature to be ready for marriage. Sometimes couples, or one of the partners, may seek professional help to consider some of their doubts and difficulties.

Here is an example from my clinical practice. Elizabeth, an attractive, lively, intelligent woman in her early thirties was to be married in four months' time. She had become engaged only ten weeks after meeting Christopher. She had been swept off her feet by his love letters, the flowers he sent her, his interest in her work. Although she had had a number of intimate relationships with boyfriends in the past, she had found those who were interesting and fun to be with had not been able to commit themselves to an ongoing relationship; others who were interested in marrying her, were boring. None had courted her like Christopher, nor been as caring and considerate. She told me that the two of them had much in common, their times together were harmonious, there was a natural understanding of each other and they were able to share their thoughts and discuss things openly, including their views on marriage and having children. They both did freelance work which they enjoyed and admired each other's work which was different from their own field of interest. Elizabeth liked and admired Christopher's family and was liked by them; it all felt right and fitting. She was excited and happy, hardly able to believe her good fortune; so when he proposed, she had joyfully accepted. She continued to feel confident—until the day the engagement was made public. The announcement was made by her future father-in-law at a party for family and friends. When the assembled guests raised their glasses to toast the young couple, she suddenly felt awful. It all seemed so formal; it didn't feel as if this was about her and Christopher but as if she was playing a role in someone else's script. And now that she and Christopher were discussing the arrangements for the wedding and where they would live afterwards, their views often differed, leading to heated arguments. When he told her that she was very opinionated, she was deeply hurt although she realised that there was truth in what he said. Every time they were unable to meet in the evenings, she now began to question whether they really loved one another. She had a dream in which she told him she was leaving and had walked away from him. She had expected him to immediately follow, begging her to come back to him and was shocked to find that he had stayed behind with his friends. They had in fact had a heated argument the previous evening and there had been no time to resolve it before they parted. She spent much of the night feeling that the link between them had been irretrievably broken. And yet as soon as they were together again the following day, she felt reassured, finding that, as on other occasions, they both had the capacity to listen to each other, consider the other person's feelings, and find a mutually acceptable compromise.

What came to dominate her mind was the worry about having to fit in with his religious orientation. He was a keen church-goer and very much a part of the Catholic community in the area. She was quite willing to have a religious wedding, was in fact born into a Catholic family but seldom went to church and had no religious belief. She could not see herself participating in any of Christopher's church activities. Indeed the thought of him attending Sunday services was oppressive. I knew that Elizabeth had until recently led a very independent, adventurous life and liked to do things on the spur of the moment. This made me say that perhaps it was not only his Sunday morning commitment but any structure that felt to her like a prison, preventing her being a free spirit, doing whatever she felt like doing. I said that to let go of the freedom to do what one fancies, and when, is in fact part of living with someone else; however, she seemed to experience accommodating to and respecting his needs as severely restricting her freedom. "And to think I'll be just a wife," she exclaimed. "I certainly won't change my name to his!" I said it sounded as if she felt an essential part of herself had to be given up and would be forced to fit in with whatever Christopher wanted. But had she not told me that they both were able to listen and respect each other's views and wishes? Yet she was afraid that marriage meant being in bondage, losing her own identity rather than a coming together of two adults who could allow differences to exist and find a way of making these the basis of a new, enriching joint life.

During the following few weeks, as both sets of parents took over much of the organisation of the wedding arrangements—which she found to be too formal, too elegant, not to her taste—she felt increasingly stressed and unenthusiastic. Her former liveliness appeared to have left her. She then had a dream that shed further light on her troubled state of mind. In the dream she had travelled to Africa and was bathing in the sea when an old man came towards her, throwing white powder into her face which attacked her skin and threatened to kill her. Having related the dream, she said that after finishing university, she had, on the spur of the moment, taken a trip to Africa, had swum in the turbulent sea, and had a great time. The white powder reminded her of a mask or make-up for a stage performance. I said that she had told me that the wedding felt to her to be a kind of show. It seemed that she felt as if she would have to put on a performance, to get into a false skin, that her true nature, her spontaneity, her adventurousness, her fun-loving part, her vitality, were being killed off by a kind of Svengali theatre director-partner, destroying her own identity.

The question was why she should feel so powerless, so easily taken over. I linked it to her having always resented her father telling her what she should and should not do. She had objected to his strict adherence to prescribed outer forms of behaviour which she felt showed no understanding of how she was feeling. She had rebelled against his edicts and chosen to lead a very different life from that of her parents, who had in fact separated when she was a young child. She felt constantly told off, given instructions which led to arguments and screaming at each other, but she could neither ignore what he said nor move away from living in close proximity to him. Nor was she able to put a stop to father's almost daily visits (putting her flat and financial affairs in order). When I asked why she allowed these intrusions, she said that he had done so much for her, she was the centre of his life, he had no friends; to erect a barrier of any kind would be cruel, tantamount to killing him. One can see how much this pattern of mutual dependency with her father led to being terrified of marriage: it meant entering into another relationship in which she was the centre of attention and care but at the price of being dominated, forced to adopt ways of being which did not accord with her own nature. It meant not only fitting in some of the time with what someone else wanted but getting into an alien skin, killing off whatever she passionately felt was important to her. What we needed to do was to distinguish between these anxieties based on the nature of her infantile relationship to her father and the reality of the relationship with her fiancé. She needed to look at the evidence: was Christopher in fact dictating how she should think and act or merely asking her to consider his ideas and let him do what was important to him? Equally, she needed to consider whether she could allow him to be different or had to insist that only her opinions had validity.

These matters had previously been worked at in her relationship with me. She had come to appreciate being listened to, being able to disagree, being helped to think about herself rather than feeling judged and dominated. One of the attractions Christopher held for Elizabeth was that he, unlike her father, was ready to listen to her and interested to understand her point of view. Yet her fear of being dictated to and criticised remained and this made her vulnerable to feeling hurt whenever there was a difference of opinion. In order to find a new way of relating, it is important to learn to differentiate between our inner picture—based on the past relationship with mother and father—and the present outer reality. Only then does the new relationship have a chance of being different and bringing about an inner change.

Further discussions with Christopher did reassure both of them that they could respect each other's different needs. They married and once they had children, Elizabeth, though not much interested in religion, began after a while to attend church services and, later, wanted her children to be given the experience of belonging to a caring community, something she had not had in her childhood.

The problems Richard presented were of a very different nature. He was a man in his mid-fifties, contemplating a second marriage. His wife had left him seven years earlier because, as she told him, "I have found a man who, unlike you, listens to me and doesn't only think of his work." Although, at the time she left him, he was enraged at her disloyalty and still felt deeply hurt and unfairly treated, he could see with hindsight that he had always been absorbed in his career as an actor, hardly ever at home or available for her and the children. After his wife left, he had, however, insisted on having the children, now in their teens, to stay at his home every second week. He had had a couple of temporary liaisons with women but also enjoyed his freedom. After a strenuous week's work, having time to potter in the garden, listen to the song of birds, walking his dog, and being with his children were the thing that he enjoyed and that enriched his life.

Four years ago he had become attached to a woman called Anna who was now living with him. She took care of his meals and attended to practical matters which he detested doing because they took him away from "higher, more important things". He appreciated that she was looking after him and valued her intellectually stimulating conversation. He took pleasure at being treated with affection but only enjoyed intercourse by having phantasies of other, seductively enticing women. It was she who was keen on having sex but this included some aspects which were repugnant to him. Living together was altogether difficult. He liked to eat when he felt like it, rest after lunch. He liked having a quiet time at home to recover from work while she liked to come and go as she pleased. He often felt criticised by her but dared not object for fear of her leaving him. He said it was impossible to have a discussion with her; whenever he disagreed with her, she just became angry, would not speak to him, left the house, not telling him when she might be back. Much of the time being together was intolerable. What disturbed him most was her attitude to his children. She did not want his children to be around, constantly criticised them, called them spoilt and irresponsible. She tended to go out or sit in another room when they were around. His children who were grown up by now disliked her and visited much less frequently than before she came to live with him. While he loved his home and children, her plan was that they should get married, move out of London and have a little home for just the two of them. He, on the other hand, had no intention of leaving London, its theatres and art world. He loved his present home, his garden, wanted to see his children and provide a place where they would feel welcomed.

It seemed that it was primarily his fear of loneliness and not being able to manage on his own which made Anna's presence so important to him. His mother's illness and subsequent death a few months earlier had left him without the love and support he had so much relied on. Her death had also brought the spectre of his becoming old more into consciousness and with it the fear of facing life all alone. He felt he loved his partner, was grateful to her for putting up with him, and needed her to look after the practical matters of the household as well as to protect him from the intrusion of some of his fans. And yet he felt irritated by her much of the time. He remained undecided: he felt he could neither live with Anna nor without her. It became clear that both of them used each other to fulfil some basic needs, admired each other's talents, could enjoy outings, but I never felt they loved each other.

After a long time, he brought a dream which seemed to indicate that he was still searching for an answer as to whether he should marry her. He dreamt that he, Anna, and the children were walking in the woods. After a while the path divided into two. He and Anna went along one path while his children took the other. Suddenly, he was overcome by panic, afraid he would never find his children again. In the second part of the dream, he was looking at a woman sitting by the hearth; her physical features reminded him of his mother. As he looked at her more closely, he realised she was a stranger, someone he did not know, and wondered what she was doing in his home. In the third part of the dream, he went back to the school he had attended as a child and asked his old teacher to tell him how to find his way home. I wondered about his need (shown in his dream) to go back to school to learn what he had not yet learnt, namely what it was to be truly loving. It was obvious that he wanted me to solve his problem for him, give him advice. I commented that in fact a part of him, his unconscious, held the answer to how to find his way home if only he was willing to listen to it. It showed him that the woman he claimed to love was a stranger, taking him away from what he valued in life, especially his children. Nor had he yet found someone that he could truly love. He gradually came to see that he had exploited Anna's affection for him to satisfy his infantile needs to be looked after, rather than loving her. It seemed, in fact, that they used each other rather than loved one another. Eventually, he went to stay with friends for a while and with their help wrote her a letter, saying he felt he could no longer bear living with her. She agreed to move out but they soon started to meet again, sometimes to go out together, at other times to provide some specific help. Marriage was never mentioned again.

Getting married always involves some losses, some relinquishments though not necessarily as great as the ones Elizabeth was so afraid of and Richard had good reasons to fear. The question is whether something essential, something that is most deeply valued, will be lost by living with a partner. Some degree of privacy and independence will certainly have to be given up, some sacrifices made, some compromises arrived at. In making plans, one is no longer a totally free agent, one has to consider how one's activities will affect the other as well as oneself: his physical, intellectual, emotional needs; her family ties; financial and other commitments. Unlike before, major decisions, as well as areas of responsibility for each partner, will need to be discussed and worked out jointly if they are not to be resented or felt to be at the expense of one person or the other. All this takes time and is often a difficult and painful process, raising questions of dominance and passivity, feminine and masculine roles, giving and taking, tolerance of differences. It can so easily lead to conflict and power struggles rather than an exploration based on interest in the other and his otherness. Unwanted, buried aspects of oneself are likely to come alive within this intimate relationship. On the other hand, differences and respect for the partner can lead to great personal enrichment, to a complementary, mutually supportive, fulfilling relationship which grows more deeply over time. Many couples are willing to work hard at understanding each other, sometimes aided by professional help. Others get divorced or continue in an unfulfilling relationship.

The traditional stag-party and hen-party prior to the wedding is a last fling at being a bachelor or a single girl amongst one's special same-sex friends. While each partner might continue to feel close to some of his or her own special friends, social life will in future primarily be in terms of relating to others as a couple. Some past friendships may lose some of their intimacy or be lost altogether.

The relationship to parents undergoes a major change. The new couple need time on their own to learn to live together on a day-to-day basis and build a home and life of their own. The highs and lows of their relationship are their private affair. Loyalty to the new relationship means it can no longer to be discussed and analysed with other members of the family as it may have been before marriage. I have often heard parents say: "I am not losing a daughter, I am gaining a son"—or "I am so happy he is getting married, I now have a daughter as well as a son". The family may well be enriched by gaining a new member but why, I wonder, do so many mothers—and sometimes fathers—shed tears at the wedding? Is it because they are touched by the beauty of it all, moved by the spiritual solemnity of the ceremony? Or are they remembering their own wedding, wishing that they were setting out once more with the same enthusiasm, hope, and happiness as they felt then? They might perhaps look back with sadness at their own wedding which was not as happy an occasion as the one they are now witnessing. They may be worried about what kind of future awaits their child. Seeing the young couple might make them feel suddenly old. It may be any or all of these thoughts which affects them. But is there not also some feeling of loss, an awareness that this event signifies some break with the past, some severing of the previous connectedness that had existed between parent and child? Although no umbilical cord has to be cut as it was at birth, emotionally it may feel to the parent just like that. Someone has come and broken the close tie between mother and son/daughter, father and daughter/son, the bonds of love and care, of attachment that reach back to before the child was born. Although their child may have had close relationships with other adults, now he has chosen someone who henceforth will be *the* most important person in his life, the one in whom he confides, whose counsel he seeks. At the end of the Jewish wedding ceremony, it is the custom for the groom to step on a glass—breaking it is meant to bring the couple luck. It seems to me that this ritual may symbolise a breakage with the past, particularly perhaps the breaking away from mother. Does the glass perhaps symbolise the baby-bottle?

My mother used to say that she was happy to have three daughters, as they tend to stay closer to their parents than sons. I think there is some truth in this. Many mothers find it hard to let go of the close relationship with their child whom they cared for, worried about, nurtured. The relationship now assumes a different form, however good this might turn out to be. There is the desire that the couple will keep in close touch and the hope that one day there will be the joy of having grandchildren. If the parent has been very close to the son or daughter, the loss will be profound and will need to be mourned. If the grief is not worked at, it will result in an interfering, hostile competition in the couple's life which is the butt of so many jokes about mothers-in-law. In reality it not infrequently leads to serious conflict. Fathers can be just as unwilling to let go of their daughters, jealous of the man who takes his little girl away, feeling himself also to be ousted from his position of authority, like the father who pronounced: "Why should I go to their house, they should come to me, I will never bow to my son-in-law". We tend to smile at a child's Oedipal desires, his wish to have one of his parents (usually the parent of the opposite sex) all to himself but tend to treat Oedipal feelings of parents in relation to their children with little sympathy. The wish to possess the other, or at least to be the one who is most loved, and the feelings of jealousy when we are not, remain and have to be reworked at every stage of life. The paradox is that the more that parents are willing to let their youngsters go, the more likely it is that the latter will want to remain in contact, although on a different, more adult basis.

In Western societies, many marriages end in divorce and the number of young people who live together without marrying has increased. Yet most young couples, even in Western countries, believe in marriage which provides a legal and a spiritual/religious commitment to each other and the children they hope to have. It provides the challenge to go on striving for a permanent relationship enriched by love that can overcome difficulties. The couple's experiences of how each partner's physical, mental, emotional, spiritual state affects the other may lead to a greater awareness that this is but a microcosm of the interdependence of members of the family and the society they live in, of the interdependence of our lives and the lives of those in other lands, of human life and the environment, life on planet earth and the cosmos, a vision of a whole interconnected world.

CHAPTER TEN

Becoming a parent

The wish to have a baby is often already present in childhood. I remember being far less interested in dolls than in live babies. The fact that I was the youngest child in my family probably had something to do with it. Did I feel dolls to be like dead babies, lifeless, worried about my mother having no more babies after me? I begged to be allowed to push the pram and spoon-feed the baby of one of my mother's friends. Pets also aroused maternal feelings: I loved Anton, my uncle's dog whom I often took for a walk and, of course, my two canaries whom I looked after and hoped they would mate and have little ones. I was very disappointed when they did not do so.

In adulthood, as well as a love of children, additional motivations enter in to wanting to have a child. There is the awareness of being part of a lifeline which stretches from past generations and makes us wish to continue it; in doing so, we may feel that we are investing in a future beyond our lifespan. Maybe there is also the hope that by having offspring, a part of us remains alive—is immortal. There may be a desire to preserve or pass on the qualities we value in our partner, our parents, grandparents, and/or others who have inspired us. Having a baby is also often felt to be a present one is giving to one's parents. And indeed a baby is usually a source of infinite joy for them as well as

103

enriching the lives of other members of the family: sisters and brothers, the newcomer's siblings, cousins, youngsters who are often thrilled at becoming uncles and aunts. Wishing to but not being able to produce a baby is felt as a failure and a very painful loss. The feelings of loss may be ameliorated, though not necessarily eliminated, by adopting a child or becoming a stepmother/father. "Stepfather" and especially "stepmother" carry such bad connotations that I prefer calling them "second mother" or "second father". This makes it clear that while the birth parent is number one, never displaced or forgotten, someone else has taken on an important maternal or paternal role.

Whether discovering one is pregnant is a source of joy or dread depends on many factors: whether the child is wanted, wanted at this time in life, whether it is an "accident", the result of a casual sexual encounter or the consummation of an ongoing loving relationship. However much desired, pregnancy brings with it fears as well as hopes. There are worries about the foetus as well as about the mother: will she be able to carry the baby to full term, will the baby be born healthy? Anxiety is all the greater when there is a history of miscarriage, still-birth, or abortion. There are fears of the foetus damaging mother's body, both while inside her and during the process of giving birth; fear of harming the foetus by not taking care of one's health by smoking and drug-taking. Some expectant mothers feel joyfully filled by the new life growing inside them; others, or the same mother at different times, may experience the foetus as an intruding foreign object. Every pregnancy has its unique character, influenced to some extent by external circumstances and the support given by the partner and members of the family. Primarily, it is coloured by the pregnant woman's history of her relationship to her mother, her mother's body, her babies; all these are re-evoked by being pregnant (Raphael-Leff, 1993; Waddell, 1998).

Here is an example. A student I shall call Ann, came to see me when she was nine weeks pregnant. She told me that she had decided to have an abortion but her boyfriend was afraid that this might damage her and wanted her to rethink her decision. She looked radiant and self-confident, saying that she had made up her mind and was only coming to please Paul. She spoke about him warmly, saying he was kind, intelligent, and they had many shared interests. He was the first person in her life in whose company she felt confident and at peace. Last spring they both suddenly had a great urge to have a baby. She had no doubt about wanting to marry Paul and he too had expressed his wish to marry her.

However, she could not tell her parents about the baby. If faced with her pregnancy they would say that it proved how irresponsible she and Paul were and forbid her to marry him. But they had to tell her parents because they needed their financial help. Ann remembered that when she was a little girl she would say to her mother: "Mummy, I am sorry, I didn't mean to upset you, I shan't do it again", and her mother would reply: "It's no good you promising, I know you will." I commented that even now she was having these internal conversations with her mother and seemed to expect that her relationship with Paul and having a baby would be seen as just being a naughty little girl. It seemed to prevent her feeling she was an adult now and needed to think about the implications of having an abortion and what it might mean for her and Paul's relationship. She reiterated that nothing could alter her decision to have an abortion and she had already made an appointment at the hospital. She told me that the appropriate time for me to help her was after she had had the abortion. I said she expected to be upset then and that my task was to pick up the pieces after the event rather than help her think through on what basis she was taking this step. I added that she and Paul clearly wanted to have a child yet I was struck by her not thinking of the foetus inside her as the first of her and Paul's children. At this she stalked out, saying she was not sure she would come next week as by then the abortion would probably have been "fixed up".

It was only at Paul's insistence that she did come for the second time. She declared that she was definitely having the abortion. I said it was still not clear on what grounds her decision was based and that I had the impression of her as a young girl engaged in a personal vendetta with me, just as if she were still fighting with her mother. Ann now told me that she had never been close to her mother; in fact, she had spent a good part of her first two years at her aunt's home. The reason for this was that her mother had become pregnant again "almost immediately" after giving birth to Ann. When this second child was born, he was weak and difficult to rear, so her mother was preoccupied with him. Ann never got on well with her brother; she always fought with him, even now. She had been told that, at one stage in his babyhood, it was thought not to be safe to leave her in the room with him without an adult being present. I said I could understand that she had been very angry at being ousted by this brother; it seemed that she had been murderously jealous and still has not forgiven him for being born. I wondered aloud whether the foetus inside her might be felt, by a child-part

of her, not to be her own baby but confused with her mother's little boy
that she wanted to get rid of. She also appeared to feel that her mother
had never forgiven her for attacking the baby brother and would not
allow her to have a baby of her own. Ann was silent for a moment and
then said sneeringly: "That's all fairy-tale stuff."

She came for a third time, announcing that she was keeping the baby
after all. She added: "This, of course, has nothing to do with our talks."
She and Paul were planning to marry shortly and he was coming home
with her this weekend to tell her parents. She thought that her mother
would, perhaps, not be "all that unreasonable". In a dream she had the
other night, her mother had looked at her swollen stomach and after
chiding her "just a little", had embraced her. I cannot be certain that my
interpretations helped this young woman to keep her baby but I tend to
think that the shift in her feelings were not unrelated to her experiences
in the consultations with me. I think it likely that the undoing of her
confusion between her own and her mother's child led to her changing
her mind. I also think that her experience of me as a motherly person,
who, although knowing about her murderous jealousy and attacks on
her brother, clearly allowed her to have a baby of her own, made it possible for a forgiving aspect of her mother to come to the fore. Having a
baby brought Paul and Ann to commit themselves to marriage and also
brought about the hope of a better relationship between mother and
daughter.

Expectant parents tend to have all sorts of phantasies about what
their baby will be like. With the help of technical advances, we are now
able to get glimpses of pre-birth life and even observe the foetus' movements at the time when ultrasound pictures are taken. These images are
bound to feed into the parents' phantasies. One mother told me that
the obstetrician had said that the foetus had a "peaceful disposition";
another mother reported having been faced with a twelve-week-old
foetus seemingly boxing in his amniotic sac. She and her husband felt
reassured at his being such a strong, lively baby—but might it also have
given rise to worrying that he would be a fighter, very aggressive? In
fact he turned out to be a baby that was determined to get what he
needed and had both a passionate and a loving disposition. Sharing
emotive experiences and phantasies about their baby during pregnancy
helps couples to understand each other in this new situation of becoming parents and is likely to strengthen their relationship. Antenatal
groups for mothers, joined, at a later stage, by their husbands, help to

prepare both partners for what will be helpful during labour and, in addition, allow them to discover that they are not the only couple that feels anxious, full of uncertainty.

Whatever the expectations and preparations, giving birth to a baby is a momentous event, a matter of life and death, of terror and fulfilment, of immense tension and relief. The emergence of a healthy baby is an occasion for pride and joy. For some parents pride at having produced a baby continues to be the dominant response. The child may be thought of as a prized possession which they expect to fit in with their way of life, their likes and dislikes, to fulfil their ambitions, and used to heighten their self-esteem. There are others who have a baby in the hope that it will provide them with the love they feel they have not been given in their family of origin. This is frequently the case with teenage mums, often themselves children of deprived teenage mothers. They are usually not aware of how much love and devoted care the baby needs and how it will affect their own education and social life. Other couples, who decide to have a baby hoping that having a child will mend their unstable marriage, mostly find that it does not.

Most couples regard having a baby as a fulfilment of their love for one another. Many experience feelings of awe at the miracle of having given life to a new human being. They hold their baby in their arms, examining his toes, his fingers, his facial expressions, delighted and amazed at finding that this tiny little infant has come into the world equipped with such complex physical/emotional/mental capacities. It fills them with a sense of wonder as well as gratitude at having been given this most precious gift. It calls forth the wish to understand their baby's unique personality and provide a loving environment that will allow him to develop to his full potential.

The infant, cut off from the source of life, warmth, constant supply of nourishment, exposed to an alien environment, reaches out with his cry, his open mouth, his unsteady movements to be reconnected to mother. While she is likely to be delighted at being so desired, she may also feel intimidated by knowing that his life, his very survival depends on her. Will her breast be able to nourish him? Will she be able to hold him safely, comfort him when he is distressed? Father too may feel alarmed at the new demands made on him. One sympathises with the young man who exclaimed: "And to think that I will be responsible for him for the next eighteen years!" Little did he realise that such responsibility usually extends far beyond that period, sometimes for a lifetime.

He told me that it was not so much the extra financial burden he was thinking of but having to be a husband and a father who, by his own example, helps his son to become a boy, a man who cares for others, appreciates all that is good in life, as well as having the strength to deal with hardship and sorrow.

Having a baby alters each partner's pattern of life, his and her sense of identity, and affects the relationship of the couple in major ways. Having more or less successfully adjusted to one another, a third person has entered into their lives, affecting whatever balance has been achieved in the marriage up to this point. This newcomer is likely to become a shared, treasured focus of their lives, greatly enriching their relationship; but for some, it may revive past unresolved conflicts experienced in triangular relationships. This was the case with one of my patients whom I shall call Mrs. Y. She was happy about her marriage but got angry whenever her husband did not come home straight after work. She was especially annoyed at his frequent visits to his sister. I gradually learnt about the exceedingly close relationship Mrs. Y. had with her father. In fact she was not only his beloved daughter but also his confidante with whom he discussed his problems at work and within the family, including difficulties with his wife. No wonder that when she gave birth to a baby girl, she became obsessed with thinking that his daughter would become more important to her husband than she, his wife and mother of their child.

I wonder how many women, prior to having had the experience, realise just how physically and emotionally demanding it is to take care of an infant, especially in the first few months; or that it takes time to get to know your baby and adapt to his needs; that to be a mother involves learning a whole new way of being. It means not only providing physical care and enjoying the infant but also being receptive and able to bear the infant's and one's own anxieties about his neediness, helplessness, and fear of dying. The capacity of mother and father to be in touch with primitive anxieties, to contain, think about them, and maintain hope rather than being overwhelmed, despairing, going to pieces, is to a large extent dependent on the way they were (or felt they were) parented in their infancy and childhood. It also depends on their having been able to imbibe from their mother and father the capacity to put meaning to their experience of emotional pain, to think about and accept it as part of life. If not, the lack of containment is very likely to be passed on from one generation to the next. I am thinking of a mother who is quite unable to tolerate her baby's crying. She and her mother carry the baby around constantly and try to avoid anything that might upset him; for instance, postponing changing his nappy though it is obvious that this is needed and feeding him before he shows any sign of being hungry. The moment he becomes restless, she goes to extreme lengths to stop him expressing his distress, stuffing food or a pacifier into his mouth and although he keeps spitting it out, she keeps on shovelling it back in. This mother was brought up on the then-current Truby King method which advocated feeding babies only at four-hourly intervals and not picking them up when they cried. As an infant, this mother had therefore not had the experience of emotional pain being contained, made bearable, and she, in turn, cannot tolerate pain, neither her own nor that of her baby.

Parenting a child is the most responsible of jobs. Not surprisingly, the strain of being constantly needed, exhausted by disturbed nights, persecuted by the baby's demands, makes mothers, at times, feel totally controlled by their infant, hating him, wanting to get rid of him. Often mothers feel too guilty, too ashamed, to talk about such feelings; yet they are universal. If negative emotions cannot be spoken about, a mother may become so persecuted by the baby that her angry feelings can be in danger of being enacted.

Yet in spite of the strain, the love, delight, and concern for the baby often exceeds all mother's, and father's, expectations, and increases as the child develops. Responsibility for the child's life can evoke qualities of love one had not dreamt of possessing. I remember hearing the story of a mother who, when she saw a lion about to attack her two young children, told them to stand absolutely still and saved their lives by placing herself in front of the lion. I was amazed at her bravery but once I became a parent, I felt I would be able to do something similar if the children's lives were in danger: to preserve their lives felt unquestionably more important than protecting my own.

Psychoanalysis, infant observation, and developmental studies have all shown that the nature of the relationship between mother and baby, of father and baby (and to quite an extent that of siblings) in the first year of life lays the foundations of the child's physical, emotional, mental development. More recently, advances in the field of neuroscience have led to the discovery that neural connecting pathways are beginning to be laid within the brain in the first year of life by loving, satisfying experiences while they fail to develop to the same extent if positive experiences are rare or absent. Bion's (1962a) concept of containment, that is, the need for the infant's inchoate, primitive feelings to be transformed by the parent's ability to understand them, attach meaning to them, make them more bearable, has been widely accepted and recognised as being vital to the baby's development of a secure inner world. On the other hand, the projection of negative, unwanted aspects of the parent's personality into the baby has serious, adverse effects on emotional development which may last a lifetime. All these aspects of interaction have been evidenced by closely observed infant observation: studying the way the baby is handled, spoken to or not, held in mother's gaze during feeds or not. But I wonder whether there is something more than what we call projection; namely, that there can be an actual transmission of a spirit of love, hope, life-energy (or its opposite: hopelessness, hate, negative energy) beyond what is observable which enters into and can affect another person's well-being, his soul. I am thinking particularly about what a decisive role such transmission of the spirit of loving life-energy may play in helping the baby's ability to bear pain, or even in the survival of a hypersensitive, exceedingly vulnerable infant, such as one born very prematurely and/or disabled. All babies are born with an emotionally permeable skin, able to sense and be powerfully affected by their caregivers' states of mind. Children, too, sense and react to their parents' and other people's emotional states. Many retain this sensitivity as adults: we intuit, sense something of another person's inner mental state. Most of us are familiar with becoming aware of the prevailing positive or negative, over-excited/manic or depressed atmosphere as we enter a room full of people; even when we visit an empty house or certain places, we may be emotionally affected: it is as if a benign or, alternatively, a malign spirit of those who have been there before has left its mark.

The capacity to transmit positive life-energy has been recognised by spiritual healers and those who turn to them for help. Such ideas are generally dismissed as pure illusion. I had a friend who worked as a healer. Once, when I mentioned that I had a pain in my neck, she put her hands gently on the back of it and I felt intense heat coming from them. It would seem that such individuals are able to gather into themselves some positive cosmic energy and transmit it to others.

In the following cases, the difficulties in becoming a parent led mothers and fathers to seek professional help. The problems they brought seriously undermined their parental capacities but they also highlight the kind of emotional disturbances experienced, to some extent, by many a parent. If these can be looked at, understood, worked at in a therapeutic encounter, a dramatic change can often be brought about in the parents' capacity to understand and contain their own and their baby's anxieties that consequently changes the way they relate to the child. A more benign cycle of interaction tends to be set in motion: the infant's loving response to the more understanding care he receives, especially his smile, gives such pleasure to mother and father that it leads to further mutually satisfying interactions.

No wonder that the provision of parent-infant therapy has become far more wide-spread and is recognised as fundamentally helping the child's development as well as that of the parents. This, as well as thera-peutic counselling during pregnancy, is indeed the most preventative mental health work. Here, as well as elsewhere in the book, I mainly draw on brief work with clients but I am aware that it is the intensive, long-term analytic work one has done—and continues to do—that makes it possible to get hold of the anxieties presented quickly.

Brief therapeutic work with parents of infants

Mrs. A. telephoned, asking for an urgent appointment, saying she was absolutely desperate because her four-and-a-half-week-old baby's screaming was driving her "mad". The secretary who answered the phone told me that the baby's scream had a very piercing quality.

I saw the parents, and baby, who slept throughout the session, that same evening. Mother told me that she feeds the baby at frequent inter-vals and plays with him afterwards but within minutes of being put down he starts screaming and she cannot get on with anything else. Having agreed that this was difficult, I asked the parents to tell me about the history of this baby. I learnt that there had been problems right from the start. Mrs. A. had been very sick during much of the pregnancy. A few weeks before confinement, the doctors became worried about the baby not gaining weight. Mother was eventually hospitalised and when there were signs of foetal distress, two weeks before the baby was due, a Caesarian operation was decided upon. The baby was lying in a transverse position and had the cord around his neck. Mother was told that he was very thin because he had not been able to get enough nour-ishment from the placenta. Father added that "he was emaciated, like a concentration camp baby—all skin and bones."

They were told to feed him every two hours. Mother's nipples got sore and she became progressively more exhausted. She wondered whether he was getting enough from her breast, so she had weaned him a week before and bottle-fed him, yet he still continued to scream whenever she put him down. She mentioned that when she is not alone in the house, the baby cries less and when her mother puts him in his cot and rocks him, he settles and sleeps longer. Mother said: "I have not got time for all that, I have to get on with work on my computer. Also my maternity leave will be up soon and they will not give me more time off nor let me work part-time. I don't want to neglect the baby and leave him all day but my career is important to me." I commented that she felt the baby gave her no peace and would continue to do so, never allowing her to resume her career. Perhaps this had led her to work at home already. Her worry about the future might also have made her tense and impatient with the baby. Mother looked surprised and asked: "Can my nervousness and wish to get away from him really affect him? Do babies pick up such feelings?" She then spoke about how ashamed she feels when he screams when she takes him with her to the shops. "All the other mothers know what to do to satisfy their babies," she said. Mrs. A. dissolved into tears; Mr. A. moved closer to her, comforted her and took the baby from her. I commented that the baby made her feel a failure. Mr. A. said: "I think the baby is trying to tell us something. We are trying to be good parents but what is the baby feeling?" Mother added: "Does he feel we are monsters? He seems so violent when he beats my breast with his fists. Can babies be violent?" I said she had no doubt that he was sometimes angry at being kept waiting for a feed but perhaps she felt that the baby's scream was a way of accusing her and avenging himself for not having got enough nourishment when he was inside her.

Towards the end of the interview, they told me that they both came from broken homes. In fact they had put off having a baby because they thought that having children had led to their parents' quarrelling and the break-up of their marriages. Clearly they feared that having a child would destroy their own relationship too. We agreed to meet again in a week's time but I indicated that they could contact me earlier if they needed to do so.

I felt Mr. and Mrs. A. to be a loving couple and observed them being gentle in their dealing with the baby but was left with an eerie feeling about the baby: was the baby so persecuted by being starved in utero that he had become a very angry, unforgiving baby, the kind of child that undermines the parents' confidence at being able to produce a good child and gives them such hell that they regret ever giving birth to him? Was he in fact a very aggressive baby who would turn into a violent child? These thoughts popped into my mind from time to time throughout the week, and made me approach the second interview with much trepidation.

When I met the parents again, they appeared far more relaxed. The baby was crying but in not too distressed a way and settled as soon as he was given the bottle. The parents were both smiling as they told me that the situation had changed "out of all recognition". Mother said she had felt drained after our interview but it was marvellous what had happened since. She reported that she spent more time in putting the baby down and rocked his cot until he was properly asleep. He often slept for several hours. Sometimes he still woke after a few minutes but if she held him for a little while, he fell asleep again. Father had got a little rocking chair for him which the baby enjoyed sitting in. Mother could put her foot on it and rock him while she worked on the computer. "I have stopped worrying about work and enjoy watching him and when he smiles at me, I feel so rewarded." Father spoke about how the baby follows him with his eyes but how sometimes, when he has been left on his own for some time, the baby seems to deliberately turn away. A moment later he added: "It occurs to me now, as I am talking to you, that the baby may be cross at having been left on his own." I said: "This may well be so and isn't it interesting to think about what the baby's behaviour might mean?" Mother burst out: "Do you really think that babies think?" She had read that it was all a matter of physical stimuli. She told me that the baby still cries piercingly when the bottle doesn't come immediately after she has put a bib on him. She then reflected that when she had breastfed him, the milk had been there right away. "It's different with the bottle—perhaps he wonders whether the food will ever come?" She looked astonished at her discovery. Perhaps thoughts about his experience in utero also crossed her mind, as they did mine. "But it's all so much better," she said. She was wondering whether she could persuade her boss to let her work part-time. She told me that she used to be very ambitious, a "high-flyer", then added: "It's not so important to me any more since I find more pleasure in the baby."

Father said: "It's wonderful what has happened since last week, we are very grateful." I asked: "What do you think did happen?" Mother replied: "When we came, I thought that I had done something terrible to him, he had such a dreadful time inside me. At other times I thought that there was something very wrong and disturbed about him, something really nasty and dangerous. I thought if he is so violent now, what will he be like when he is five, ten, fifteen!" I said that she had been afraid that they had produced a child that was full of destructiveness.

Mrs. A. said: "I think we were selfish, we had such a good life, just the two of us, we wondered whether the baby would put an end to all that. We wanted him to fit into our lives and not take over; instead he did take over and controlled us. I was both angry and frightened and it all got into a vicious circle. We are on a much better footing now. I feel easier, he feels happier and I feel so happy that I can make him happy." They again expressed their gratitude and said they would write to me in a little while to let me know how they were managing. They sent a letter two months later in which they stated that the baby was happy and contented; mother was working part-time and granny was looking after him while she worked. "Far from spoiling our relationship," father added, "he has become a joy that we share and also helps us to get to know each other in a new way."

I believe that at the first meeting some of the parents' persecutory anxiety about being monsters was relieved and this enabled them to make some sense of the baby's piercing scream. In our second meeting, I was touched at their starting to observe and understand their baby, seeing him as he really was rather than as a violent child who was destroying their life. That fear had been projected into me and was temporarily firmly lodged there. It made it possible for them to take a genuine interest in the baby, observe him, think about his emotional state in context not only of what had happened but also what was happening now. It enabled mother and father to take better care of him, feel rewarded by his response and increasingly understand him and enjoy the relationship. Trying to deal with the difficulties had brought the couple closer together.

Although a number of factors combined to make it hard for Mr. and Mrs. A. to become parents, some of the difficulties are ones that apply more generally. The arrival of a baby is bound to limit the time a couple has for each other, restrict their freedom, and often will affect the woman's career for a considerable period. These inevitable losses encountered in making space for an addition to the family are likely to arouse some frustration and resentment and this, in turn, may lead to feelings of depression and guilt. Feeling deprived of what they enjoyed before is usually more than offset by the interest and pleasure in getting to know a new, developing person, being able to be the provider of the baby's needs, to make him happy. If negative feelings, anxiety, and depression become paramount, they will be conveyed to the baby; the less physical and emotional holding is provided, the more anxious, upset, demanding the infant will become, thus confirming the parents' worst fears of not being good enough and/or experiencing the baby as a tyrant.

Loss of princess status and lack of support

Mrs. B. was referred to the counselling service by the health visitor who stated that she was concerned about the baby being frequently left unattended. Mrs. B. came to her appointment dressed from head to foot in white. Her beautiful, long, blonde hair and pale make-up completed the picture of virginal perfection. She told me that she had come to England as an au pair and soon found herself being courted by the son of the family she worked for. Within months they were married and had much fun together, partying and going out a great deal.

The physical changes brought about by pregnancy—"no longer having a girl's body"—were felt by Mrs. B. to make her look ugly. After the baby was born, she had put much energy into regaining her previous figure and looks. She felt terribly lonely, imprisoned in the house during the day and left with the baby in the evenings while her husband frequently went out with his pals. It made her feel that he and his friends were cold and uncaring. She missed the lively company of her girl friends in Hungary with whom she had shared phantasies of travelling around the world, meeting and being admired by an attractive, wealthy Mr. Right. Mrs. B. began to cry. I said I could understand how angry and devastated she felt at all these wonderful young girl expectations being shattered. Moreover, she seemed to have to bear these painful feelings all on her own. She said it was good to be able to talk about it. I commented on how hard it was for her to be so far from home, without the support of her family and friends.

Mrs. B. came to her next session dressed entirely in black. She said that since talking to me, she had been feeling miserable and had cried a lot. Until then, she had just felt very angry, betrayed and had wanted to try to get back to how things had been before she had the baby. She spoke about missing the warmth of her family and friends; she was planning to visit them with her baby at Christmas. She had in the past found herself angry with the baby when he cried and just left him to it but had now become aware that he was even more unhappy than she was. She now found herself comforting him and in doing so she also felt comforted. His loving response was so rewarding, it made her feel that she was important after all—although in quite a different way than she had previously thought possible.

I believe that being able to put her feelings into words enabled Mrs. B. to begin to come to terms with her anger and to mourn the loss of her idealised self and the ambitions associated with this self-image. Finding her unhappiness being listened to by a sympathetic, concerned motherly person, enabled her, in turn, to be in touch with her own and her baby's sorrow and become able to comfort him. In doing so, she found a new, important, and satisfying role for herself. While her relationship to the baby steadily became more fulfilling, a great deal more work remained to be done to bring about a better understanding between husband and wife.

Mrs. B. may in many ways represent an extreme case, yet there are many child-bearing women who experience great anxiety, and some-times anger and depression, at the changes their body undergoes and who, once the child is born, resent the limitations that looking after the baby imposes on their social life. Being at home, alone with the baby much of the day, which is the experience of many women in Western societies, easily comes to feel like being imprisoned, cut off from adult company. If neither a husband nor family and friends are available to support the mother, it can become too much to bear.

Loss of identity

Mrs. C., a single mother, told me that people used to regard her as a superwoman. She had been in charge of a thriving business, loved organising, managing staff, supervising new employees. She was happy and in control of her life. It was all so different from how she was feeling now. During her pregnancy she had read lots of books on childbirth and child rearing and had thought she was well-prepared for motherhood. Now, however, she felt utterly helpless and useless, especially when her baby daughter would not settle at the breast, spluttered and sometimes choked during feeds and at other times, when whatever she did failed to calm the baby. "I don't know what is the matter with me," she said. "I feel confused, bewildered, frightened and helpless, it's so unnerving. All my self-confidence has gone. I cannot remember ever having felt at such a low ebb, so depressed. For the first time in my life, I cannot manage." I commented on how miserable she felt, especially as she had been so efficient up to now, and how shocked she was that reading about babyhood and child rearing was insufficient to help her deal with an actual, alive baby. I said that most new mothers find the early weeks, in particular, difficult and strenuous. I spoke about it taking time to learn from experience about what a baby needs. I sympathised with her feeling bewildered and worried. I asked whether she had attended antenatal classes but she had not done so. Nor had she kept in touch with the health visitor but thought she might do so now. We talked about her difficulty in asking for help, that she felt she ought to be able to manage on her own. I suggested that she might like to come to see me with the baby and that we might try to observe the baby and think about it together. This she accepted and it proved to be helpful.

Although Mrs. C.'s determination to do it all on her own was very pronounced, she was also giving voice to what many new mothers, especially women who are used to competently managing others' lives, as well as their own, feel when faced with looking after their baby. The care of an infant is a very new, very different and disturbing experience. There are no ready answers; organising, managing a set timetable is impossible in the first few months; the baby's rhythm and his upsets do not yield to control. It makes many new mothers feel that they have lost the capacities they had come to rely upon and to doubt that they have anything good to offer their infant. Tolerating uncertainty until one has learnt to understand and respond to the baby's communications may be hard, especially for those mothers who have repressed and are afraid of their own infantile self.

Loss of prince status

Some weeks after the birth of his first child, a patient whom I shall call Mr. D. found himself impelled to have an affair with one of the attractive young girls he met in the course of his work. They had had some flirtatious encounters and he had taken her out for dinner but he had managed to resist going to bed with her, feeling this would be a betrayal of his wife. He told me that he loved his wife but no longer found her sexually attractive; in fact he felt uncomfortable at being physically close to her. It was particularly her breasts, enlarged by feeding the baby, that he found ugly and off-putting. In his sessions with me he reported dreams in which little gnomes were pouring poison into a well and messing up a high building. We could understand his dream as arising from his anger and jealousy that his beautiful wife was no longer his sole possession. The little gnomes represented babies whom he had in his phantasy made the carriers of his attack on her body, babies who were felt not only to be sucking at the breast but spitting and urinating into it. Mr. D. now remembered being told that when his younger sister was born—he was eighteen-months at the time—he had turned away from his mother and had been fussy about food. His destructive feelings at being ousted from the position of being the little prince owning mother's beautiful breasts (it would seem in a sexualised manner) had never been worked through and were powerfully revived now that he had to share his wife with his baby daughter. It had led him to seek out a young woman, whose breasts were "unspoilt" by a baby.

Witnessing the intimacy of a loving feeding relationship easily evokes in us our infantile longing to be held, fed, cared for like the baby. It is only in as far as we have been able to mourn this very unique relationship we once had—or feel we should have had—and have learnt to share mother's bounties with a third person, father, sibling(s), that we are able to watch without feeling overcome by jealous and envy.

Post-natal anger and depression

I saw Mrs. F. five times and shall give a very abbreviated account of our meetings. She came to see me when her baby was nine months old and immediately dived into telling me about the terrifying experience she had had when giving birth to her daughter. The baby got stuck in the birth canal and when every other effort failed, suction was used to extract her. Neither the epidural nor other anaesthetics had been effective, and so Mrs. F. was in great pain throughout. She lost a great deal of blood, needed extensive stitching, and was severely bruised. She experienced the whole process as pure torture. The staff at the hospital tried to encourage her by telling her that she was strong and brave while friends she had spoken to afterwards passed it off as "just a difficult birth". None of this had been helpful: "On the contrary," Mrs. F said, "it showed me that no one appreciated how ghastly I was feeling." When

I said that she wanted me to understand how shocked and terrified she had been, perhaps afraid that she might die, Mrs. F. looked at me intensely. She told me that she was still suffering from the consequences of the birth. The episiotomy had left her so damaged that she recently had to undergo laser treatment and only now was able to resume having sexual intercourse. "I know it's irrational, but I blame the baby for all this," she said. "My husband and all the family adore the baby and they can't understand why I cannot bear to be near her. For months, I kept on thinking: there is this little bundle that I am supposed to nurse, feed, clean up, love—but I cannot. I just want to go away and have nothing to do with her. Every time I look at her, I am reminded of the terrible time I went through giving birth to her." I spoke about her anger with her daughter who she felt had nearly killed her, about her murderous feelings towards the baby but also about her wish to protect the infant by having her looked after by a good child-minder rather than attending to her herself. I felt her to be deeply depressed, full of hatred and revenge towards her child but also profoundly guilty at harbouring such thoughts.

She asked to see me again soon and we fixed an appointment for four days later. She looked a little brighter and told me that talking to me had been very helpful, especially my saying that she had been terrified that she would die. She said this was absolutely right and it was so good to have this acknowledged. She had been able to look at the baby more and feel less angry. In the course of some months, Mrs. F.'s anger abated, her depression lifted, and she was gradually able to be close to her daughter and even begin to enjoy her company.

At the end of our five meetings she said: "If I had not come to see you, I think I might have seriously harmed the baby or killed myself." There had been some doubt in my mind whether it was safe to end our meetings but I felt that I could trust her to contact me again if she needed to. The question as to whether a few sessions are enough is always a problem when seeing clients for only a brief period. She asked me to write to her doctor to tell him that if she ever got into such a state again, he should refer her to this clinic rather than treating her with medication which had not helped her.

Post-partum depression, whether leading to withdrawal and misery or permeated by anger, is not an infrequent occurrence and may have many complex sources arising from the past as well as the present. Severe depression needs to be distinguished from the universal depressive feelings which arise from loss of the physical union with the baby during pregnancy and/or reliving one's own infantile separation from mother. Although most women in the last few weeks are impatient for the infant to be born there may, all the same, be feelings of loss, an awareness of an empty space within the body. We are all familiar with depressive feelings from other occasions when a deep involvement in a creative endeavour comes to an end—the end of a project or the day after an enjoyable, festive event for which one has spent months preparing.

A father's post-natal depression

Mr. and Mrs. G. were referred by their doctor as there was concern about Mr. G.'s drinking which sometimes led to aggressive behaviour towards his wife. Mr. G. sat down next to me while his wife took a seat across the room, hugging their six–month-old baby. Encouraged to tell me about their problem, Mrs. G. indicated that it was really up to her husband to take the lead. Although his initial response was to say he was not used to talking about his feelings, they soon came pouring out: how he felt there was no longer any place for him at home, that his wife was no longer interested in him. He tried to be helpful about the house but he felt so rejected that he had taken to going out with his chums in the evenings. Sometimes he got drunk and then he could be "rough with the missus". His wife sat through all this, smiling and cooing to her baby. I commented that she was showing me that she was completely wrapped up with her baby which was indeed a wonderful thing to behold but it seemed to leave no space for her to think about her husband or want to include him. As Mr. G. continued to speak about feeling miserable at being unwanted and unloved, his wife began to listen and to look at her husband with some concern. She said: "But I do love you, I think I'm just too tired when you come home to talk about what has happened with me and the baby during the day or to want to hear about what sort of day you had." When I encouraged the couple to tell me about their families, I learnt about mother's sister who had always been very close to their mother and remained mother's favourite. I commented that she perhaps wanted to recreate this closeness with her own baby but this left her husband feeling left out and miserable, just as she used to feel as a child.

By the time they came to their next appointment, both Mr. and Mrs. G. looked happier. They reported that following our conversation, they had talked a great deal and this had made them feel closer than they had for months, and father had not been drinking so much. Mother said that she now gives father the baby to hold when he comes home. Father spoke about how much he enjoyed giving his daughter a bath and playing with her and both he and his wife sang to her when they put her down to sleep.

Mothers of young infants are bound to be primarily preoccupied with their young babies but sometimes this can amount to disregarding their husbands' needs. Fathers have to come to terms with no longer being the main focus of their wive's attention and at the same time have to bear the brunt of the impact the baby is having on mother's physical and emotional state. They may accept that their main role at this time is to support their wives but can easily be made to feel that the contribution they are making is not sufficiently appreciated. If, on top of this, they are excluded from taking part in looking after the baby, competition with the baby and envy of maternal capacities can easily be exacerbated and get in the way of being a loving father and husband.

Summing up

Becoming a parent inevitably involves some sacrifices for each partner but the pleasures and satisfactions, the joy and enrichment, of having a child usually far outweigh whatever (at least for some time) has to be given up. Caring for an infant has the potential for furthering our own psychic development. As one mother told me: "I always thought about what I could get from others and it was never enough. I now find that giving myself to the baby and seeing that I am able to make him happy makes me feel so different, so much better. It has changed my whole outlook on life. I realise now that giving to others makes for inner happiness." The young child's curiosity, excitement, and sense of wonder as he discovers the world around him gives us another opportunity to be aware of the extra-ordinariness of what we may have come to accept as ordinary; and while trying to meet the needs of the child, his unique personal qualities have the potential for re-awakening as well awakening new aspects of our own psychic life. This is how one father so touchingly expressed it: "With each child we had, a new part of my heart opened."

I am aware of having written about what is still generally considered to be a normal family constellation. There are some gay and some lesbian parents, many single mothers, divorced couples, second marriages, sometimes with both partners already having children, and other highly complicated family situations, but these are beyond the scope of this book—indeed it would require another whole book to deal with them.

CHAPTER ELEVEN

Bereavement

We are confronted almost daily, via the media, with pictures of men and women, in one corner of the world or another, distraught at the death of members of their family and friends. Such brief, voyeuristic intrusion into grief to which adults as well as children and adolescents are exposed, may shock, horrify, make us aware of the unpredictability of such tragic events and the frailty of life but does nothing to bring us any closer to understanding the complex, inner turbulence that follows upon a death. We remain unprepared for the powerful emotions we experience when someone close to us dies and are at a loss to know how to relate to those who are bereaved. I remember a friend of mine, in a senior position in his social work organisation, who lost his wife suddenly, unexpectedly, telling me that his colleagues scurried away like mice when they saw him coming along the corridor. When staff had to consult him about work-related problems, his wife's death was not even mentioned by them. When I asked them why they had not said anything about his loss, some replied that they had not wanted to intrude; others felt they did not wish to upset him and some said that they did not know what to say.

It is true that there are no words to adequately express the gravity of what has happened but surely some acknowledgment, voicing how sorry we feel, sending a card or offering some practical help, would at least show that we care about what has befallen the person. Is our avoidance of the bereaved due to not wanting to be "infected" by depression, to get upset, to be touched by pain and closeness to death? When the loss is spoken about, platitudes which do nothing to comfort the bereaved, are often uttered, such as: "It's over now" or "It's for the best" or "Think of what she has been spared". Unhelpful advice is also frequently proffered: "You should try to get away from it all … travel … move house"; as if a change of location, some distraction, would rid us of the pain. We seem to do anything to avoid giving time and space to listening, being in touch with the feelings of the mourner.

Those in so-called "caring professions" are often no better at dealing with the feelings aroused by death. I vividly recall being in hospital very many years ago when a woman, in the bed opposite mine, suddenly collapsed and died. The nurses rushed to her, pulled the curtains around her bed, put out all the lights in the ward except, of course, the one by the woman's bed where there was a great deal of ongoing activity. We were told to go to sleep—and, to my surprise, some patients did so. Was their withdrawal into sleep the only way to escape from the shocking reality? It was the first time that I had been present at someone's death. I was frightened and alarmed and had a need to talk to the person in the bed next to mine but when I did, was firmly told by Sister to keep quiet. I did not sleep much that night; I was thinking about death and also about the woman's husband being given the news and how he would feel.

Let us consider some of the painful states that tend to be experienced when someone we love and/or depend on, dies. The immediate reaction is shock. It manifests itself physically as well as emotionally: feeling cold, numb, dazed, disorientated, going about aimlessly, acting like an automaton. Such reactions will be all the more pronounced if the death has been unexpected; for instance, when it occurs as the result of an accident, a heart attack, or a stroke. When one is present at the death of one's dear one, it is incomprehensible that one minute there was a person and the next there is only a body, the physical shell left. Where has the soul of the person, his spirit gone? It is a mystery. Every religion holds that the soul is immortal but where and in what form it may go on existing within the universe we do not know.

Even when the death has been expected, the finality of the loss and our total helplessness in the face of it leaves us shocked and bewildered.

People who are in a state of shock need physical and emotional warmth, need to be relieved of any practical obligations not connected with the person who has passed away. They need to have the possibility of talking to those they feel close to, people who are sensitive, aware when their presence is wanted and when the bereaved need time to be quiet and on their own, though knowing there is someone nearby and available to turn to. I can hardly bear to think how impossibly difficult it must be if the person who is bereaved has no one with whom to share his feelings nor anyone to help look after him. If we have not been present at the death of someone close to us, we want to know exactly when it happened, how the end was, what the person said, felt, whether they were conscious, in pain—hoping to hear that the end was peaceful, fearing to learn that it has not been so.

"I don't believe it", "Surely, it's not true": such spontaneous exclamations on learning about the death of someone with whom we have had a close relationship, expresses our attempt to deny the stark fact, the finality of the person having gone forever. It is too shocking, too painful to absorb; our mind, our heart, does not want to take it in. There is the external loss and the inner state of feeling an emptiness, a void, an essential part of oneself having gone and leaving a gaping hole. The world seems unreal. I remember that after my first analyst died, the houses in the street looked, for weeks, as if they only had a surface, were insubstantial. Participating in the planning of the funeral service (and the funeral itself) brings home the reality of the person having gone but at least we can do something which will honour him or her and do it in the spirit of the departed. A funeral or cremation is usually, but not always, accompanied by a religious service, even when the deceased has not attended a house of prayer for years. In addition to the minister, some members of the family or friends may want to speak. I remember a cremation at which the service consisted entirely of the playing of pieces of music that the deceased had especially loved, each person being left with his own thoughts about the person who had gone out of our lives. That too was a very moving event.

For quite a while, the mind tends to refuse to fully take in the awful truth: we may mistake a person in the street, wearing a coat like the one our husband wore, for the one we have lost. We may wait for the sound of the door opening and for our loved one coming to greet us; at times we may sense his presence in the room. The feeling of unreality is increased if the death occurred in a far-away country. It is even more difficult to be in touch with what has happened if the body is missing, for example, lost at sea or as a result of an air-crash. Often, the relatives have a need to visit the site of the disaster and mark the spot in some way.

We may accuse ourselves: "If only I had not let him work so hard" ... "I should not have allowed him to use his bike at night" ... "I should have insisted on her going to see her doctor earlier." Such comments express the belief that one could have prevented the person's death. Self-accusations will plague us most intensely if there has been a suicide—we feel guilty at having failed to notice the seriousness of the depression, the anger, the desperation, the hopelessness that drove the person to take his life. Some feelings of guilt are common after every death. We may feel that we could have done more to make the person's life easier, happier, better. We are ashamed if we have quarrelled, said something hurtful when we last met, feel that we should have been more considerate, shown more care, visited more frequently when the person was ill or lonely. We may regret that we have neglected to show our appreciation for what the person meant to us, gave to us, failed to express our love, our gratitude; that we never apologised for hurt inflicted in words or actions. And now it is too late to do so and also too late to tell him we are sorry and ask to be forgiven.

"Why didn't he look after himself better?" "Did she not care enough for me to try to stay alive?" "How could she do this to me, desert me?" Such feelings of anger, causing us to blame the person who died for having left us, abandoned us, may be stirred up in the depth of the mind, however unreasonable they may be known to be. Anger is often directed against doctors and nurses who are felt not to have done enough to save our loved one's life or to have spared him suffering. Frequently, anger spills over into sudden angry outbursts towards others in the mourner's environment. Some people curse fate, rail against the unfairness of life or against God who failed to protect our dear one's life and is making us suffer.

(The Holocaust undermined many people's belief in the existence of God. If there is a God, they say, how could He let this happen? But this assumes that there is an almighty God, responsible for our and other people's crimes. It is human beings who do not respect human life, are greedy, envious, project their own destructiveness onto others, blame them for the ills of the world, and engage in what is ironically referred to as "ethnic cleansing".)

Most of the time we do not acknowledge, do not allow ourselves to be conscious of the fact that life is transient; that bad things happen also to good people, to innocent children. We too readily take our health, other people, life itself for granted and believe we should possess them forever. It is often only when we lose someone we love and/ or were dependent on that we begin to realise how lucky, how privileged we have been until now. Death can make us aware how precious life is, learn to appreciate, be grateful for what we have had and what we still have.

Freud (1917) wrote of the state of mourning: "It is only because we know the cause ... and that it will eventually pass, that we accept the state of mourning as normal rather than an illness." He described it as characterised by "cessation of interest in the outside world" and viewed the work of mourning as consisting of "the testing of reality which proves over and over again that the loved one is no longer there". He stresses the psychic energy needed to let go of the "libido" (loving feelings) attached to the person from whom one has been parted.

Karl Abraham (1924) stated that the successful outcome of the work of mourning depends on the internalisation of the loved person, that is, the firm establishment within the internal world of the externally lost one. If loving feelings predominate, he will remain as an inner presence which still enriches us and may be turned to for comfort and counsel. For instance, Mrs. V. had many "conversations" with her husband. She would find herself thinking: "Now, what would John have thought about this, what would he have said to the children, what would he have done in this situation?" Such inner dialogue with a loved person who lives on within us adds a valuable dimension to ongoing experiences. Surprisingly, it is a fact that the greater the love that united us, the more possible it is to deal with the loss. But what happens if the relationship to the deceased has been a very ambivalent one or if we remain dominated by anger at having been deserted? Instead of carrying within us a helpful, loving presence, we may be left with a hostile, accusing inner voice, turned against the self. Freud speaks of this mental state as carrying within us "the shadow of the object", resulting in melancholia as distinguished from normal mourning.

Klein pointed out that every loss evokes earlier losses in life. She agreed with Freud that the pain experienced in the course of the work of mourning is due to the necessity to renew the links in the external world and thus continually to re-experience the loss but added that the poignancy of the loss requires us "to rebuild with anguish the inner world, which is felt to be in danger of deteriorating and collapsing" (1940, p. 354). This means that not only has the support, love, and security provided by the deceased person gone forever but it is also feared that he has been lost as an internal supporting presence, leaving the mourner feeling empty, chaotic, sometimes afraid of going mad. It evokes catastrophic anxiety of utter helplessness, of not being able to survive on our own, as in our infancy. The fear that nothing good will survive within our inner world is closely linked to the resentment at the pain and suffering that the loss has imposed on us. We are then afraid that our love for the one who has left us will not be strong enough to preserve the goodness of what we have been given by him or her in the past.

The bereaved person needs others to show him love and concern. This goes some way towards helping us to feel we are not left totally abandoned; it reassures us that there are others who care for and who love us. Relatives, friends, members of the community one belongs to, may provide loving care. Some religious rituals incorporate this. For instance, in Jewish (and Hindu) communities, not only do people assemble for prayers morning and evening at the mourner's house for seven days following the burial or cremation but they also visit the mourners at other times during the day, bringing food for the bereaved and their family. Such gatherings allow for the sharing of each person's memory of their contact with the deceased, bringing home to the mourners that there are others who have loved and valued the person who has gone from their midst and who will keep him alive in their minds. The work of mourning takes a long time and while some of it needs to be done privately, sharing it with others, especially those who have suffered losses of a similar kind, can be of great help.

Whatever help is given initially, it is important that the bereaved person is not forgotten but continues to be thought about and, in so far as he wishes, drawn into the company of others. Sleeplessness, anger, depression, mood swings, loneliness, yearning for the person lost—all these will beset the mourner over a long period. Indeed the loss is never wholly overcome. The scar of loss remains and the wound opens at anniversaries, festival times, and also at unexpected moments. Grief can, however, easily turn into self-pity; it may lead us to become passive, expecting others to take care of us forever instead of trying to take our life into our own hands, to wake up, to act in a way that gives it a new meaning. What makes a memorial event, the gathering of those who have loved the person who has gone from their life a few months or a year earlier, so valuable is that it allows us to share our memories with others, to think of the kind of person he was, what he achieved, what we have gained from his view of life, his way of dealing with fortune and misfortune; in some cases even the positive way he dealt with illness and dying. It may make us try to emulate him.

The eventual outcome of mourning depends on whether we remain resentful about being robbed of someone we feel should have been there for us forever or whether gratitude for having known him and having been enriched by the relationship supersedes our deep hurt. Being parted by death puts to the test whether we regard the love and support we have had as our birthright or as a gift that we are fortunate to have received, for however brief a time. If it is the latter, we will remember the person with love and try to continue to value what we have learnt from him. This may take the form of carrying on the work the deceased had been engaged in, and/or striving to emulate his good qualities. It can lead to appreciating life more and having greater empathy with those who suffer physical or emotional pain. Some individuals are moved by the tragic loss of a dear one to engage in a project that helps others to be relieved of unnecessary suffering, like a lady I know who supplied a hospital with newly discovered medical equipment to help to diminish the kind of agony her husband had had to endure.

I have sometimes heard people criticising a bereaved person (behind their back) for behaving in what they consider to be an inappropriate way. They might, for instance, say that he or she should not be going to a party so soon after someone's death or wearing bright clothes. I feel strongly that we have no right to prescribe to others how to manage the extremely painful experience of loss. Each person needs to find out for himself what makes it possible to bear the extremely difficult, frightening thoughts and emotions, the loneliness that follows the death of his dear one.

There is cause for worry only if in the long run there is an inability to face the work of mourning. Some people, unable to accept the fact that the beloved will never return, keep everything that belonged to him as if he were still alive. Queen Victoria for many years insisted that Prince Albert's bed was made ready for him each night and his day-clothes laid out for him each morning. Some parents keep their child's room unchanged for years after he has passed away. It arises from the dread that if the outer signs of his existence are not held onto, one will be left with an utter, unbearable void. I have found Steiner's (1993) distinction between "fear of loss" and "experiencing of loss" helpful in this context. It is only when we can admit to ourselves that the person has died and let go of possessing him that we will be able to fully experience the loss and be able to establish him within our inner world. That requires an act of faith.

There are others who attempt to banish the deceased from their minds, quickly dispose of anything that could act as a reminder. I know a young father, who, almost immediately after his wife's death, threw all her clothes in the rubbish bin, tore up her letters and any photographs in which she appeared. He would not allow his wife's name to be mentioned in front of the children nor did he ever speak of her to them or to his friends. He felt so hurt, so angered by her death that he wanted no reminder of the life they had once shared. This made the loss threefold: he lost his wife, he lost her within his inner world, and he lost the capacity to feel deeply about others. His character hardened, he ignored his children's emotional needs, and was unable to engage in any but casual relationships. He worked ceaselessly, accumulating possessions, surrounding himself with all the latest luxuries but found no real pleasure in life. It was his feeling of inner emptiness when his business was declared bankrupt which brought him (and his inner bankruptcy) into analytic treatment many years later.

Feelings of guilt may in some cases never be overcome: "I should have noticed that he was not well"…"I didn't visit her when she was so ill" … "I should have been there when he died." These thoughts continue to haunt. Some bereaved people experience guilt at regaining joy in living, feeling their pleasure to be at the expense of, a triumph over, those who have died. Ongoing deep feelings of guilt may lead to hyperchondriasis, the mourner harbouring within himself an ill and dying object which needs attention. Others may become accident-prone as a way of punishing themselves. I remember an adolescent boy who had gone to a football match in spite of his father having urged him to visit his granny who was expected to die any day. Next morning he learnt that she had passed away in the night. A few months later, he stole a bicycle in full view of a passing policeman. He was clearly asking for punishment in order to atone for his guilt. Nothing leaves us feeling more guilty than a death by suicide. We feel we should have been more observant, more aware of how depressed, angry, hopeless the person felt; how he hid himself from view, did not communicate. How could we not have noticed and if we had, could we not somehow have prevented him from taking his life? But there may also remain anger at what a young person has done to his parents by killing himself, their child, trying to make them feel guilty forever. The suicide will affect the siblings and the feelings of hopelessness and anger in the face of life's difficulties may be passed on from one generation to the next.

Some individuals, finding grief too hard to bear, continue to fill their days with frenetic activity or turn to drink or drugs. Manic behaviour may be promoted by friends of the bereaved. For instance, in the weeks following the death of her dearly beloved father, an adolescent patient of mine told me that she was having "the time of her life". She was showered with presents, taken out to restaurants, and generally made a fuss of by her parents' friends as never before. Such running away from depression may be a way of providing temporary relief from overwhelming pain but if it persists it will result in shallowness of affect, a turning to material satisfactions rather than engaging in relationships and risking being hurt so deeply again.

Far more frequently, we meet people who are unable to emerge from feelings of lasting or recurrent bouts of severe depression, unable to find resources within themselves to face life without the other. Some question, or assert: "If there is death at the end, what is the point of life?" I tend to think it is rather the other way round: it is the very fact of having limited time that makes us aware of life's preciousness. Although our human life is finite, we are part of the infinite life in the universe and the way we lead our life contributes to or diminishes the life of other humans beings, as well as playing a part in the preservation or destruction of the earth itself. Some who have lost hope may seek therapeutic help to discover what has happened within their shattered internal world and what is hindering their recovery.

The death of one's child is felt as the most terrible loss of all, most especially if it is one's only child. It is a life we have helped to create and have invested with hope. A miscarriage, a stillbirth, the death of a baby, some too prematurely born, shakes the mother's belief in her maternal capacity to carry, give life to, nourish a baby, to make him thrive. Every such loss needs to be mourned rather than replaced by quickly becoming pregnant again. I have had patients whose mothers' repressed mourning interfered with relating to their new, alive child who in turn felt burdened by mother's unavailability and never felt wanted for his own sake. To lose an older child or an adolescent may be even harder to bear. We have begun to see him develop, expected to see him fulfill his potential, hoped he might be happy and creative; hoped he would one day provide us with the joy of having grandchildren and make us feel part of a continuing chain of life. Every time the parents see other children, other adolescents, young people getting married, it brings to mind what their own son or daughter would have been like at that stage of life had he or she lived. And as the parents get older, the absence of the younger generation becomes even more painful. It is equally painful for older people to lose their grown-up son or daughter. It feels as if the natural order of things has been reversed and a permanent, most painful scar is left. Yet some parents find the strength and generosity to engage in work or projects which make safer, and enhance, the lives of other children, other adolescents, other young people. I particularly remember the parents of Suzy Lamplugh—the young estate agent who disappeared in 1986 after meeting an unknown customer—who set up a trust which highlights the risks people face and offers advice, action, training, and support to minimise such risks. It continues to be used by police and the government. I know parents who not only published the drawings of their artistically gifted daughter, killed in a terrorist attack, but in addition set up a foundation to help to preserve the sight of children in India and thus enjoy beautiful things as their daughter did. In this way, parents and others who engage in such reparative projects following the death of a beloved relative, find some comfort in knowing that what they do will save and enrich the life of others. It gives their own lives, in memory of their child, a new meaning.

Bereavement at different points in the life cycle

In childhood

Losing a parent severely shakes a child's sense of security. In addition to losing the person the child has depended upon, it undermines his belief in the reliability and strength of adults. It inevitably arouses the fear that the other parent will also die. Following his mother's death, a five year old was overheard talking to his older brother at night. He was anxiously asking: "Is daddy going to die now too? Are we going to be sent to a home?" Fortunately his aunt was within earshot and tried to reassure the child, saying that daddy was not ill like mummy had been and they would never be sent to a home, that she and all the other members of the family were there to help to take care of them.

The dilemma for young children is that they are not yet able to distinguish between phantasy and reality. They believe their thoughts to be omnipotently powerful and thus angry thoughts are felt to do actual harm to others, not only within their mind but in the external world. If mother or father (or sibling) falls ill or dies they often feel themselves to be the cause of it: "I was very naughty, that's what made mummy ill and die," four-year-old Maureen said. Five-year-old Freddy told his teacher with utter conviction: "I killed daddy, I know I did because in my dream I pointed a gun at him and shot him dead." Eight-year-old Johnny, unable to deal with his frightening feelings of guilt, blamed his younger sister for causing mother to die and attacked her mercilessly. It is not uncommon for such children not to want to go back to school. This may be due to their feeling insecure and worrying about the surviving parent's safety but children also tend to feel embarrassed at being different from others and being held responsible for what has happened.

If one of the parents dies, the surviving spouse may be so wrapped up in grief that he or she becomes inaccessible to the children. The children thus experience a double loss, missing the attention and understanding they so much need in order to deal with their complex feelings of fright, confusion, and insecurity. Children in a house of mourning can be such a comfort to the surviving parent, bringing hope for ongoing life and growth. I think of seven-year-old Jill who seemed to convey this to her grieving father when she pulled him by his sleeve, saying: "Look daddy, I have got a new tooth!"

When one of their children dies, both parents may be so preoccupied with mourning the child they have lost that there is little or no room in their minds for their other children. The lost child is often spoken about as having been the best, the most gifted. The jealousy and envy this can evoke in their children may add to their feelings of guilt about the death of their sibling, as well as cause them to feel unloved themselves.

I remember seeing a six-year-old little girl a few weeks after her baby brother died. Mother brought Geraldine because she refused to go to school. On the few occasions when she was able to drag her there, the school nurse would ring an hour later, asking mother to collect the child because she was crying and could not be consoled. When they came to see me, mother told me how she had found her baby boy dead in his cot when she came to his room one morning. Geraldine was not at home at the time as she was staying with her granny for the weekend. While mother recounted the story of Sam's tragic death, she cried bitterly; in-between sobs, she was telling me how beautiful, delightful and charming a baby Sam had been, such a joy! Meanwhile, Geraldine was drawing a picture of stars in a dark blue sky. She was glancing from time to time at her mother who was totally absorbed in her grief. I was vividly aware of how excluded Geraldine was feeling but at the same time felt great sympathy for this mother and wished to allow her space to speak and share her grief. Geraldine now held up her picture to her mother but the latter was lost in thought and unaware of her. I turned to Geraldine, saying that there was one star that was especially big and I thought she wanted to be that star that could make mummy be bright and happy again. As mother continued to cry, Geraldine took the black pencil and fiercely crossed out the biggest star. I said that when mummy was so sad and thinking so much of baby Sam, she felt *he* was mummy's special, bright star and that she was not as important to mummy as him. It made her very cross and want to get rid of her star-brother. I also said that when she was at her granny's, she might have felt angry that he was at home with mummy and had her all to himself. And now going to school may also feel as if she is being sent away, that mummy is at home, not thinking of her but only about Sam. Geraldine looked at me with big eyes. Mother looked astonished, called Geraldine to come to her, held her tight and kissed every part of her body. She now cried both for her baby and for Geraldine on whom she had unknowingly inflicted so much pain. Two weeks later Mother let me know that our meeting had helped both of them to feel closer again and that Geraldine was able to go to school without too much difficulty.

Many parents fail to realise how important it is to let children participate in mourning rituals and make it possible for them to ask questions as well as to answer them in a way the child can understand. Parents may refrain from doing so, believing that they are sparing the child pain, but the adults' upset is bound to come across to the child anyway. To be excluded from what is happening will only result in filling the unknown void with phantasies more terrifying than the reality. Sometimes the untruths that children are told increase their anxieties. Here are some of them: "Grandma went to sleep", may make a child afraid of going to sleep; "Mummy has gone up to heaven", has made many a child afraid of blackbirds or stars, believing that they are the dead parent watching and judging their every action from above; "Daddy has gone on a long journey", must sooner or later lead to wondering why he has not come back. Does he not love us? And when the child discovers that he has been lied to, his trust in the adults telling him the truth is bound to be undermined.

In adolescence

For many teenagers, standing as they do at the threshold of exciting new opportunities, death may seem a long way away. Many take great risks. It may be their fear of being able to deal with adult life and responsibilities that drives them to expose themselves to dangerous situations. It comes as a terrible shock, however, if one of their friends commits suicide or dies as a result of drug-taking. One adolescent I saw for therapy had lost a boyfriend who had been a drug addict. She herself continued to be heavily involved in drugs. It was her way of making herself feel high rather than confronting her misery; nor was she able to face the fear that she too might die. Such feelings were projected into me, filling me with great worry and fear for her safety when she continued to boast about the drugged and drunken states she got into. The situation came to a head when she produced a knife in one session and stood poised to attack my throat, laughing while she did so. When I said that I was the one who was to be terrified of dying, of being killed, she put the knife down and it became possible for the first time for her to listening to me speaking about her difficulty in holding thoughts of danger and death in her mind.

Adolescents who lose a parent face special difficulties. Just as they blossom, their parent loses his or her life. If the one who died is of the same sex, the adolescent may have to take on some aspects of the role of the deceased parent. For instance if the father dies, the boy may feel—may in fact be encouraged to feel—that he is now the man in the family, the one mother needs and relies upon. In so far as this is felt to be a fulfillment of his Oedipal wishes to oust father and take his place, this puts him into a frightening position. It leads to feelings of persecuting guilt as well as arousing fears of being too close to mother. Robert, a boy I saw a year after his father's death, had dealt with the arousal of sexual feelings towards his mother by attacking her physically in quite a dangerous way. Others in this situation may defend themselves against such feelings by running away from home or seeking a homosexual relationship. Girls who lose a mother may face an equally difficult situation, often being thrown into looking after father and the younger children. The extent of unconscious feelings of competition with mother will determine whether this is experienced as just being helpful or as a manic triumph over mother, leading to guilt. In either case, taking on too many adult responsibilities may become too heavy a burden, interfering with the enjoyment of youthful freedom.

Losing a parent of the opposite sex may, on the other hand, pose the problem of mother and daughter, father and son becoming more like siblings, sharing many activities, competing for social contacts and partners of the opposite sex. Such youngsters often feel too guilty to go out with friends, have a good time, or move away from home, fearing they are deserting their lonely parent. If the parent finds a new partner, it often arouses great hostility to the newcomer and the feeling that father or mother is being disloyal to the deceased.

In middle age

In addition to feeling bereaved, the loss of one's parents may result in the links to the past, to one's wider family and culture, being lost. It is too late now to ask questions, to discover more about the previous generation's life and to find out the identity of the people in the old family photo albums. There is an awareness that the buffer that one imagined stood between oneself and death has been removed; one is now a member of the older generation, the one next in line to die. Thoughts of one's own death add to the depression of losing a parent. But such thoughts may also make one appreciate the brevity and preciousness of life, weigh up what one wishes to, needs to, and can do, in order to use the time one is still granted.

This was not the case with a lady in her late fifties who came to see me some time after her husband's death. She said that her children were wonderfully supportive but she couldn't bear it when they or their friends mentioned her late husband because this made her cry. He had been such a good man and they had shared so many interests. He had died from a heart attack while they were on holiday abroad. She continued meeting with her group of bridge players several times a week but they too were not allowed to mention his name. She spent the evenings looking at photos of her husband and feeling bereft. I came to feel that that she was trying to keep him to herself, owning him. It made me ask whether she ever talked to him while she looked at the photographs. She answered that she never did. I put it to her that she was in a way imprisoning him inside her instead of relating to him and allowing others to do so too. She seemed to accept this and began to speak to him when looking at his photo, talking about their life together and how she missed him. It brought about great relief. She was then able to let her tears come and soon also to allow others to share their memories of him, even when it made her burst into tears. Gradually, she began to enjoy her social life and after a while found a partner. She had no intention of getting married again but she enjoyed his company and affection, though, as she assured me, the relationship was nothing like the one she had had with her husband.

In old age

People in their old age are likely to suffer bereavements more frequently. They are left feeling more and more lonely. The death of friends of their own generation also leaves them without others with whom to share memories of events and people they all knew. Recording one's life history may become an important task, a way of remembering as well as preserving something of one's experiences and what one has learnt from them for the next generation(s).

If one's partner dies, it may loosen the bereaved partner's bond to life. It is therefore not uncommon for the spouse to die within a year after his or her partner's death. To want to stay alive requires the capacity still to appreciate the beauty of the things that surround us; to enjoy children, grandchildren and other young people, a creative activity; to continue to be interested in what is going on in the world; perhaps even to go on pondering the meaning of our own finite existence within the framework of the infinity of existence.

CHAPTER TWELVE

Retirement

Men and women who find their work uncongenial, too burdensome or too exhausting, often long for the day they will be able to retire—hopefully with a pension. There are others who are eager to begin a new kind of life, to move to a different place and/or to devote time to other treasured activities. And there are some who may wish to continue working but, in accordance with the rules of their employment, have to retire when they reach a certain age. What tends to be overlooked is the pain that many—even those who wish to retire—feel at the losses sustained by retirement. The emotional upheaval experienced is often unexpected and tends not to be spoken about, perhaps because it is embarrassing to admit that one feels ambivalent about retiring when everyone expects you to feel happy at gaining freedom from the burden and restrictions which work imposes. Moreover, being of an age that leads to retirement inevitably makes one aware of becoming old.

In Western society, we define ourselves and are defined by others to a large extent by the work we do. One of the first questions many people ask when they are introduced to each other is: "What do you do for a living?" To have to say: "I am no longer working, I am retired" may feel as if one is no longer an interesting person. As work takes up the greatest part of most people's waking hours, retirement brings about a very major change and poses questions. How will I spend my days? What do I want to do? What do I need to do? How will I spend the rest of my journey through life? Many people do not prepare themselves for their retirement, some have vague ideas about their future, few have well thought-out plans. Retirement can be a dangerous time for workaholics who have used work as a defence against inner turmoil; they may break down mentally or, more often, physically once they have stopped working.

Some immediate reactions following retirement

I remember feeling full of joy and gratitude on the day after my retirement party. I wanted to phone everyone who had been there to thank them for having given me such a wonderful, memorable, fun-filled farewell. I had already thanked them but still felt I wanted to do so again. Yet later I wondered whether this urge to be in touch with all the people concerned was prompted by the fear that, from now on, the contact I had enjoyed with so many others might cease. When one of my colleagues told me that she had been asked to chair a new project, it brought home to me that I was no longer eligible for such a task. Nor was I any longer in the position to influence the development of the training courses or the future of the organisation.

The following morning, I awoke thinking that in my leaving party speech, I had omitted to say how important the sense of belonging, being part of the Tavistock Clinic, had been for me. At that time, the Tavistock ideals were, to a great extent, my professional ideals. It was my work-home and now I had lost this place that had been so much part of my life. I had lost the professional community, daily interactions with colleagues, stimulating meetings with them as well as with students. I had welcomed the students' questions, for they helped me to clarify my own thinking, and to witness the students' development was a great joy. All these losses were only beginning to hit me now. I had denied them before, stressing to myself and in conversation with others that, as I was going to continue doing at least some bit of work at the Clinic, I was not really leaving. But being a "visiting teacher", not an inherent part of the core group, not part of its daily pulsating, stimulating lifeblood, not involved in shaping its future, was very different from the position I had hitherto held. It was immensely sad to fully face that I had to give up so much of what had been important to me. I also sorely missed having a specific room to work in and a secretary to help me! I had to let go of my possessiveness, of "my Tavistock", to face my envy of those younger than myself taking over. I realised that I needed to turn inwards and outwards, to try to discover what I still wanted to achieve, consider what was still possible for me to do as well as keeping up past connections and hoping to develop new ones. But at that moment these were ideas that carried little conviction of being achievable. Although I had plenty to do—and knew how fortunate I was to be able to continue with a bit of my work at the Clinic as well as my private practice and some teaching in other countries—I felt a deep sense of loss.

A colleague told me that she was going to leave her job some months before she reached retirement age. It made her feel it was her decision rather than that she was being made to leave because of age. She felt gratified when her colleagues expressed their appreciation of the contribution she had made to the work of the team and said that they would miss her.

One week after she had left, she went back in order to clear out the papers she had left in the drawers of her consulting room. She was surprised to discover how disturbing an experience it was. Her name had already been removed from the door of her room. It felt as if she had been wiped out! She found it difficult to decide which papers were no longer relevant and should be disposed of and which to keep for further use. While she was engaged in this task, she could hear the voices of other members of staff, assembled in the room next door, discussing their work. She suddenly felt extremely hungry, "starved", had a sore throat and felt generally unwell. Once she left the Clinic, all these symptoms disappeared as suddenly as they had come. It seems that the sorting of papers and feeling excluded from the staff meeting next door evoked a very painful awareness of wanting to hold onto the past, of having to let go of much that she valued—a task we have to undertake at every point of major change. The psychosomatic way she experienced the losses, points to their origins in infancy and childhood. The sound of the voices next door brought home to her that she was no longer enjoying the mental food that they were sharing. It stirred up infantile anxieties of being starved and a childlike longing to sit at the table, sharing the food that the parents and siblings were having. Might the sore throat and feeling ill be physical manifestations of an angry, inner screaming at not being allowed to partake of what the others were enjoying next door? Having to let go of past good experiences had evoked deep-seated feelings of being alone, excluded and separated.

Long-term reactions to losses at retirement, being made
redundant, unemployed

Loss of employment

Whether one's work is satisfying in itself or merely a means of earning a living, being employed implies that one is doing something that has value, as evidenced by getting a monetary reward. It means being needed, wanted, and creative in one way or another. Being out of work, retired or made redundant, leaves the person without such reassurance and may result in him feeling useless, superfluous, no longer needed or valued. For some, the job may have carried with it status, prestige, power—all these will now have to be relinquished. In as far as the person needs these external crutches to make him feel important, he may suffer a severe loss of self-esteem. To some extent, we all remain children at heart: wanting to be loved, seeking the recognition, approval, praise of parents, teachers, siblings. Their absence may result in feelings of worthlessness or at least doubts about one's worth. Retirement may feel like being ousted, not wanted, or no longer fit to work. Feeling rejected in turn tends to evoke resentment, jealousy, and envy of those taking one's place and is part of the work of mourning needing to be done at that time.

Loss of structure

Those who have made definite plans for the future may be happy that they can now do what they feel passionate about. For others the freedom they have dreamt of enjoying once they retire often turns out to be double-edged. There is the pleasure at being relieved from the pressures of work, of rigid timetables, of having time-limited holidays. But once one has enjoyed an extended period of rest or holiday, how does one deal with unlimited freedom, the loss of structure of the day and week, the absence of defined tasks and goals? With no outer structure to hold onto, does one have the discipline to use time constructively, creatively, thoughtfully—or is time squandered? When left to choose what to do, does one experience a feeling of emptiness, a lack of purpose, boredom? The very freedom forces the person to confront his inner world, to consider his priorities, what he values and what gives his life meaning. Experiencing being cut off from his work environment, he may feel bereft, lost, without anchor. Retirement is also bound to lead to reviewing what one has achieved, and failed to achieve, in the course of one's life hitherto. Guilt at having neglected what should have been attended to while employed and regret at missed opportunities, are part of such a review. Moreover, one might in the past have attributed not getting on with particular activities to a shortage of time but now discover that one actually lacks the capacity to do them—such as completing a project, playing a musical instrument, painting, writing a thesis, sport of various kinds. All kind of fears, doubts about oneself that were kept at bay while one was busily occupied, tend to surface and can no longer so easily be pushed out of one's mind.

Loss of companionship

In the course of our work, most of us come into contact with a number of people: work-mates or colleagues, secretaries, bosses, clients, customers, patients, caretakers, canteen staff, members of other organisations. With the event of retirement most, if not all, of these work-related social interactions are lost, depriving the individual of the stimulation, interest, and comradeship they had provided. Even some of the irritations, the disagreements, and verbal fights one had might be missed, since they added spice and liveliness to daily life! If he is lucky, the retired person remains in contact with a few of the people who have become friends. If he goes back to visit his former place of work, people may greet him in a friendly manner, be pleased to see him briefly, but he soon realises that they are busy getting on with their own lives, their relationships, their concerns about the work in which he no longer plays a part. It makes him acutely aware of being separate, on his own. Once he accepts that there is no way back, his current social life comes under scrutiny. Are there good friends, close family relationships to make one less bereft of company? If the partner is working, one may be alone all day. The insufficiency or inadequacy of close relationships becomes more apparent. Single people may become more aware of not having a partner to alleviate the loneliness, to communicate, have fun, share worries with, to provide support. If there are no children or grandchildren who come to visit, the silence of the house is more acutely felt.

Married couples may have to face the fact that the largely separate lives they had led while working may have allowed them to avoid difficulties in their relationship. Now that they are spending much of their time together, these become more obvious and harder to tolerate. Can one bear to be with one's partner all day long? Does one share enough interests? Is there space for privacy? Does one have to account for any time spent out of the house? The whole nature of the relationship undergoes a great change and may put the marriage in jeopardy. Alternatively, the marriage may be strengthened by joint activities, the appreciation of each other's needs, strengths, good qualities, and the support each provides the other; this is often only achieved after a period of tension, irritation at the partner's habits, different tastes, and aims in life.

The spectre of ageing and decline

Retirement is a sharp reminder of approaching old age. One is a pensioner or an "old age pensioner", now often more kindly referred to as "senior citizen". True, there are some advantages attached to this status and one may still feel full of energy, be in good health, and engage in enjoyable activities—perhaps even develop talents which had lain dormant—which there was little time to pursue before. But worries about the future, about ageing, loss about sexual attractiveness and potency, about physical and/or mental decline, easily come to mind. To escape depression, some older men (and women) engage in sexual adventures, preferably with much younger partners, take up new, risky activities, for instance gambling or car-racing, or lead a frenetic life. The future is indeed uncertain. How much time is there left? Will it be a process of gradual, graceful ageing or will one have to suffer prolonged sickness and disability? Will there be anyone who needs us, takes care of us when we can no longer manage on our own or will we be left all alone in an uncaring society? Will we have sufficient financial resources to maintain a reasonable standard of life? Until this point in time, old age and death may not have been seriously faced. Retirement brings all these thoughts to mind and makes us realise that the larger part of our life is over.

Facing the truth that our lifespan is limited may heighten our appreciation of being alive. It may induce a greater feeling of connectedness to nature, to life in all its various manifestations, a greater commitment to do what is in our power to preserve life and care for others as well as for the environment and the kind of world we are passing on to our children and grandchildren.

Case illustrations

Let us look at how three very different individuals struggled with the emotional upheaval aroused by retirement. Brief therapy can be as helpful at this time as it is at other times of crisis, provided there is no major long-standing history of severe disturbance. The very fact that a life-changing event has stirred up deep-rooted feelings makes them more available to be looked at and worked on. This makes it possible, in even a few sessions, to bring about a better understanding of what the person is going through when he loses the working life he is used to. If the loss is not worked at, it may lead to ongoing depression, illness, or dependency on drugs and alcohol.

Mr. E., a consultant ophthalmologist (eye-surgeon) came to see me a few months after retiring from his hospital work. He developed a serious illness after retirement, so he was now considering cutting down, and eventually giving up, his private practice. He felt very depressed at thinking how empty his life would be without the work he loved. "I have no hobbies, my work is my life," he said. He told me that he was not able to reduce his private work as he had not found anyone suitable to take over his practice. He spoke about this at some length. I wondered whether the difficulty in finding a suitable replacement might in part be due to his reluctance to let someone else take over his work which, as he had told me, was all-important to him. He did not respond to this but instead went on to tell me about his work in the hospital and how difficult the last few months there had been: "I was no longer consulted, my colleagues behaved as if I had already left." At the end, they had given him a grand farewell party; there had been many speeches, praising his skills and achievements. He had no doubt that the compliments were sincerely meant and was aware that his colleagues held him in high esteem. All the same, he experienced them as not sufficiently appreciative of what he had done. This was shown by how they behaved after he had retired; they had acted in ways that deeply hurt him. For instance, he had recently learnt that colleagues who had worked on a research project that he had initiated, had published their findings without ever mentioning his name. He had also heard that certain procedures he had pioneered were no longer being adhered to. I said he felt that his colleagues were no longer acknowledging his contributions—in fact felt free to steal his academic work—nor, by discontinuing to work in the way he had trained them, were they showing respect. I said that I could understand how angry and hurt this must make him feel. But as he went on speaking, I sensed that there was also something beyond these specific, indeed very upsetting, issues: a general feeling of him and his work not being remembered at all, being killed off. So I said that I wondered whether he also resented that his colleagues made changes and whether he had hoped that what he had discovered and taught should be adhered to, kept alive.

When I saw Mr. E. again, two weeks later, he told me that he had thought a lot about what I had said about wanting to be remembered. He had become aware that he had somehow hoped, even expected, that his work and name would live on, perhaps forever. "I have to learn to be more humble and accept the reality of what I have created," he said. "I know some of it was good and some of it even very good but I suppose all one does is to discover more about the body and all its incredible complexity and one adds just a bit more to our understanding of it. I have been thinking how lucky I was to have had the opportunity of a good education, excellent teachers and to be able to build on knowledge inherited from previous generations." I suggested that he could think of himself in this way too, as a link in a chain, passing on his insights to those who came after him and that something good he had contributed both as a teacher and a physician was not all lost. I said I felt that there had been a big shift in his perspective, from wanting to be so important that nothing was ever to change to feeling himself to be one in a line of those who contributed to the understanding of the human organism, part of an amazingly complex mysterious order that still needed further understanding.

We had three more meetings over the next six months. By then Mr. E. was doing much less work, having found a very able young man to take over his practice. I commented that finding it possible to hand over, letting a younger person come to the fore, was intimately linked to his being able to give up the need to assert that he was irreplaceable. He said he had been gratified to learn that his patients spoke warmly of him, calling him "a human being who cares". I said that the caring help he had given to his patients was a great gift and clearly something they continued to remember and treasure. I asked what aspects of his work he missed most. He said that he liked teaching and research but what he really enjoyed was that while he was dealing with his patients' eyes they talked about their lives; he loved hearing about these.

Having defined that his interest in his patients' lives was so important to him, Mr. E. was able to begin to wonder whether such satisfaction could be found through engaging in some activity which fitted his present circumstances. Within months, he had become deeply involved in visiting and giving advice to residents in old people's homes, reading to those who had gone blind, organising fund-raising events for homes for blind people, and giving lectures. Feeling part of a group that cared for people provided him with many of the pleasures that had enriched his life before retirement. He also told me that he had started to participate in his wife's artistic activities. He had never done this before. It made him feel closer to her; it was such a different world, one he had never known much about. He had clearly found a new life in which he could use his interest, care, and love of others while being much appreciated. I also believe that the understanding that a caring therapist provides can help a person who feels as low, as uncared for, as unappreciated as did Mr. E., to regain self-confidence. This makes it easier to invest in new activities rather than feel the future is to be a void.

Mr. P. was referred by his doctor who was concerned about his heavy drinking. He was a small, stout man with a protruding stomach. He seemed pleased to have the opportunity to speak about himself although, as he told me, he could not imagine how mere talking could help. This is his story. He had come from a poor but loving family and left school when he was fifteen to become a machine operator in a tool-producing factory. The work was boring but it left him free to talk with those working near him. They exchanged news about sporting events, gossiped about women, about domestic squabbles and the like. He said that he and his work-mates had fun together both on the job and while going for a drink afterwards. He used to come home tired, to have a meal with his wife, would watch television and sometimes go to the pub. His children had long ago left home; he saw them and the grandchildren occasionally. He had got tired as he approached retirement age and had looked forward to stopping work. But once he had left, he found it hard to have nothing to do. The days seemed long and boring. He began staying in bed longer; what was the point in getting up? He felt in the way in his own home, seeing his wife hoovering under his feet or dusting around him, so he went down to the pub in the hope of finding male company. But then he began to drink more, eventually taking some bottles home. His wife had found them hidden in a cupboard. They now had frequent rows, mainly related to the shortage of money and the way he spent so much of their limited income on drink.

I said it all sounded very sad: he seemed to miss having a structure to the day and the companionship of his work-mates, and in addition he seemed to feel a nuisance at home, unable to offer something worthwhile to his wife. "Yes, he said, "I used to come home and tell her the latest gossip from work and she would like that. Now there is nothing to talk about. I also feel I am no longer useful, my pension is less than I had reckoned it would be. I'm just in her way, a mouth waiting to be fed." I said he seemed to feel guilty at not providing as much money as before, being a burden to his wife, and suggested that he was trying to run away from these painful feelings by going to the pub. When I asked whether he had made any friends at the pub, he replied "Although we joke a lot, the guys I meet there are just like me, bored and miserable." I said he had tried to drown his sorrow in drink but this did not work for long and only made him feel worse afterwards; it led to wanting to blot out his depressed feelings by drinking more and more. I was impressed by him having been able to tell me so clearly what troubled him and wondered whether he might be able to share some of his thoughts with his wife. This idea did not appeal to him at all; it clearly did not accord with his views on what a man, a husband, should be like.

When I saw Mr. P. again, he seemed even more depressed. He had gone to visit his mates at the factory but although they had greeted him in a friendly manner, they had been busy and were chatting about the new manager and new machinery. He realised that they had moved on and he felt himself to be intruding, a hanger-on. Their talk about the firm's impending Christmas party further heightened his feelings of exclusion. Recognising that there was no way back to the past was extremely painful for Mr. P. but it was also the first step in coming to terms with the reality of his position and considering the future rather than trying to escape into drunken mindlessness. I said that I had the impression that his view of himself seemed not to extend beyond being a factory worker and bread-winner. Now that his circumstances had changed, he felt as if he had nothing to offer. He thought about this for a while and then said he was good with his hands and had in the past done some carpentry, perhaps he could take this up again. He left in a thoughtful mood.

When we met again four weeks later he looked less depressed and more neatly dressed. He told me that he had got out his tools and made some shelves for the kitchen. His wife was pleased with them. I said it occurred to me that perhaps he could use his carpentry skills to teach others to do woodwork, perhaps his grandchildren. "No," he said, "we don't see much of them."

At our third meeting, he told me that he had discovered there was a youth club down the road from where he lived. He had gone there one evening and had offered to teach some of the youngsters to make things out of wood. The youth leader had been very welcoming and he now went there twice a week. He had been asked whether he would befriend two fatherless boys and he had agreed to do so. He liked young people, was happy to help them, and last week he had brought them home and his wife had given them a meal. I commented how his new occupation made him feel that he was doing something worthwhile and was something that gave him much pleasure.

By the time I saw Mr. P. two months later, he had acquired a small allotment. He was growing vegetables and flowers. He had got the two boys he had befriended interested in helping him. He reflected that growing things made him aware of how dependent we are on rain, sunshine, the changing seasons. He had also come to see how much people depend on each other; the boys needed him and he needed them. I commented on his new awareness of the interdependence of human beings as well as man's interconnectedness with nature. He then spoke with great feeling about how flowers grow, blossom, wilt, wither, but not before they have produced seeds which in turn became plants and flowers and take up the space which has become empty. "It all makes sense," he said. I wondered aloud whether what made sense was seeing his life as one of sowing seeds, caring for the environment and the next generation so that they could blossom—and that this also made it possible to accept becoming older and eventually wilting and dying. I was deeply moved by the mental-emotional-spiritual growth of this man who had previously had such a very restricted view of his existence, had seen himself merely as a tool in other people's lives. Now he felt himself to be helping to create, promote, and sustain new life. Being in touch with nature had led to a deep respect for the natural order of growth, blossoming, decline, death, and renewal of life. He knew he was subject to this same life cycle and seemed able to accept that one had to make space for the new generation to flourish.

Miss M. found herself becoming seriously depressed a year and a half after retirement. She had been a lecturer and had enjoyed writing. She had continued to attend professional conferences and on several occasions had been asked to contribute to them. But lately such requests had been sparse and this had made her feel she was no longer wanted. She thought people now felt her to be too old, too out of touch with current thinking to be able to produce anything of interest. Even worse than this was the fact that she herself was dubious about still being capable of doing well. When she was recently asked to give a talk, she had at first been happy to accept the invitation but then became extremely anxious, wondering whether in fact she still had the capacity to write something new, well thought-out, and to present her paper in a lively enough manner to hold the audience's attention. I commented that she seemed to be anxious that her vitality and mental ability were diminishing. She said that this was her greatest fear. I learnt that her mother, now in her eighty-ninth year, had been a highly intelligent woman but in the last few years had deteriorated physically and mentally. Miss M. was worried about her mother becoming incapable of living on her own and talked to her about moving into an old people's home. This suggestion was, however, met with an absolute refusal. Although Miss M. knew that her mother was very lonely, she rarely visited her because she lived a fair distance away. I wondered whether perhaps she also avoided seeing her because it frightened her to think of herself becoming like her mother. Miss M. said every visit to her mother left her depressed, so she supposed what I said was right.

Miss M. then told me of her interest in antique Chinese paintings. Her mother and father had lived in China for some time and had brought home some beautiful works of art. It was the delicacy of the brush-work and the story they conveyed in such a simple, subtle way which Miss M. particularly admired. She was considering whether to enrol on a painting course. She also wanted to visit China but wondered whether she dared do so. It seemed to me that she was trying to make links with her parents' past life and expressing her appreciation of what they had given her. It emerged that her father had not only loved paintings but also been a gifted amateur painter.

Miss M. did in fact join an educational tour of China. She came back having had a very interesting and exciting time in congenial company. She said she found it hard now to be on her own again. This had made her more aware of how lonely her mother must feel. She had been to see her more frequently, both to share what she had seen and learnt on her trip and to hear more about her parents' life in China. They had looked at old photographs and shared memories of the past. Miss M. had visited some old people's homes but was shocked to see how most of the residents just sat and stared into space. She did not wish her mother to be similarly cut off from life and was going to arrange for her to have more help in order to make it possible to stay in her own home as long as possible. She had also spoken to the headmistress of her niece's school and asked whether her mother could be on the list of old people that sixth formers visited as part of their community project. She knew her mother would be happy to receive young people and would be stimulated by them. If her mother got frailer, she was considering bringing her down to live in a sheltered flat near her own home. Respect for her parents, identifying with her mother's loneliness in old age, and the wish to make reparation for having neglected her, seemed now to be guiding her actions. She had also made plans for her own life. She decided to enrol both on a painting class and on a Chinese language course. She realised that Chinese was a very difficult language. Learning to speak and write it would be a challenge and keep her mind active. She felt altogether more alive and was looking forward to embarking on these new ventures.

Finding a new, meaningful life

We have seen how the three people described eventually began to reshape their lives in ways that were felt to give them new meaning. The preliminary task was to distinguish between the actual losses sustained at retirement and the anxieties to which these had given rise. In Mr. E.'s case the main fear centred on his work and being forgotten; for Mr. P., feeling himself to be useless, superfluous; Miss M. was afraid of loneliness and losing her mental capacity. These anxieties resulted in depression, a lack of hope and confidence to invest in a new, different kind of life. Having to let go of the past and finding it difficult to invest in the present is characteristic of the work of mourning. Klein (1940) stated that every external loss evokes fear of losing goodness within one's internal world: loving, supporting parents/mentors and parts of the self. Feelings of loss frequently appear in nightmares: losing a brief-case or handbag which contains all one's valuables may possibly be linked to the fear of having lost or losing valuable aspects within oneself. Dreaming of losing keys perhaps may be associated with fears about having lost the key to what is felt to be home, knowledge, and understanding; loss of jewellery may sometimes be associated with the fear of having lost physical/sexual attractiveness. There is no dictionary of "this" meaning "that". It is all a question of what free associations come to the client's/patient's mind in relation to their dreams or actions. It is only when the underlying anxieties and the hopelessness about the loss are faced and put against the reality of what is still available to do and to enjoy that new strength and hope are able to come to the fore.

Being more aware of our limited lifespan encourages us to consider our priorities and to pursue the goals that we wish to, and can still, achieve, internally as well as in our relationships to others. It may also awaken an interest in our roots and make us appreciate the richness of wisdom we have inherited from previous generations. Being in touch with our vulnerability may bring with it a greater capacity to empathise with and try to help others who are needy and lonely. Acknowledging that we are mortal causes us to feel helpless, infinitely small and unimportant and yet at the same time makes us conscious of the fact that what we do or don't do, and the way we convey our love and concern, makes a difference to other human beings, to the environment, to future generations—as well as, indeed, to the poverty or richness of our own lives. Perhaps surprisingly, living a fulfilling life makes it more possible to accept that we shall one day die.

CHAPTER THIRTEEN

Growing old and facing death

"All the world's a stage,
And all the men and women merely players:
They have their exits and their entrances ...
... Last scene of all,
That ends this strange, eventful history,
Is second childishness and mere oblivion,
Sans teeth, sans eyes, sans taste, sans everything."

This is the grim picture of old age Shakespeare paints in a monologue from *As You Like It*, sometimes known as the "Seven Ages of Man". It is true, of course, that becoming old raises the spectre of loss of physical and mental abilities, going on existing "without" so much of what one had before. We know that even if we escape severe chronic physical and/or mental illness, our bodily strength will diminish with increasing age; our sight, our hearing, our mobility, our short-term memory is likely to be impaired or possibly lost altogether. We may have to put up with pain and dysfunction of some part or parts of the body. Not only do we have to face our own decline and death but also often that of our partner and, frequently, the loss of our home. But in spite of all this, does old age, even very old age, have to be "sans everything"? While we are prone to becoming needy and requiring physical assistance—in many respects similar to young children (and, if we are very incapacitated, to infants)—this does not necessarily have to go hand in hand with becoming childish. Nor must some loss of memory be equated with being oblivious of happenings in the inner and outer world. Advances in preventative medicine have extended the number of years people expect to live and new technology has helped to alleviate some, though by no means all, of the pains and physical disabilities of the elderly. Yet the fears associated with old age have not diminished. On the contrary, longevity makes us more fearful of living for years in a depleted state. There is the added anxiety that we will be left isolated and lonely, for the times are past—in the Western world—when spinster aunts and uncles as well as grandparents became part of the family household.

In *King Lear*, Shakespeare shows us an old person's agonising inner state, as he fights against the loss of power, status, and strength, demanding flattery and submissiveness. The feelings of helplessness and hopelessness in the face of decline and death can, as with King Lear, lead to one becoming dictatorial, exerting tyrannical control in order to counteract feelings of powerlessness; raging against one's fate, planning revenge against those who are felt not to show enough caring love. Shakespeare shows that this way leads to lies, feelings of persecution, a lack of trust in anyone. We have all met old people who exhibit such traits and are full of complaints (the conversation at meetings of elderly people has jokingly been called an "organ recital") but some of us have also had the good fortune to encounter old people who have continued to grow in emotional strength, wisdom, and love, right up to the moment of death. Some show great courage and achieve serenity at the last moments of their lives. The question therefore arises: what makes it possible to accept the transience of life, to bear increasing losses, face the loss of one's own life, and yet go on growing, gaining, or at least maintaining, emotional and spiritual strength?

It would seem that what is required in the first place is the capacity to let go of omnipotence and possessiveness and instead to attain humility, gratitude for the love and the life we have had and for all that is still available to us. The struggle to let go as well as to integrate the destructive aspects of self—such as envy of the young—may be especially hard for some who have held positions of power and achieved great success in their younger days. On the other hand, gratitude for the richness that life has provided in the past may make it easier for some to face increasing physical limitations as well as to accept that their life is nearing its end. I have had the good fortune to have known some individuals whose appreciation of the beauty of nature and of the miracle of so-called ordinary, simple things in life, which we tend so easily to take for granted, has been heightened in their old age.

A few years ago I met with a group of men and women in their seventies and eighties who welcomed the opportunity to share their thoughts and feelings about the challenges of old age. In the course of getting to know the individuals within the group, I learnt that every one of them had suffered one or more serious losses: losing their country of origin and with it the culture they were brought up in; losing a parent at an early age; losing a child, losing a partner; losing all those friends with whom they had shared memories of their past lives. I believe that their experience of having been able to mourn previous losses enabled them to address the losses that ageing had brought with it so openly and to think about the difficulties to be encountered on the journey of life that still lay ahead. Each individual had his or her own particular anxieties about the future but one thing that we all feared, more than anything else, was losing our mental capacity. "As long as my mind is O.K.," everyone was saying, "life can be worthwhile". Yet to be fully aware, mentally and emotionally in touch but imprisoned in a non-functioning body, unable to move or speak as a result of a major stroke or in the later stages of motor-neurone disease, seems to me equally terrifying. As I listened, it struck me how severe mental and physical impediments stir up anxieties first experienced in infancy and early childhood: being unable to communicate what one needs, wants or does not want; unable to understand much of what is happening; being helpless, afraid of dying; fearing not being understood, not kept in mind; having decisions made about one's life without being consulted. In addition to the fear of losing one's mind or control of bodily functions, there was the dread that one would be remembered in this deteriorated state rather than as the person one had been before being struck down by disease, disabilities, and all the shortcomings which we may suffer in old age.

As well as the fear of the pain and handicaps one might have to endure, we spoke about the dread of becoming a burden to family and friends. We all wished to remain useful and needed. This was equated with being appreciated, while being needy caused us to fear that we would be felt to be a nuisance, tolerated rather than loved or, worse still, being left isolated and lonely. It became clear that in as far as the old become less able to contribute to family, friends, and society at large, they are plagued by doubts about being valued; it goes hand in hand with viewing oneself as useless and unlovable. While we treasured our independence, we realised that we did need more practical help and longed for physical and emotional support, especially when undergoing intense physical and/or emotional distress. In fact, we could not imagine how we could have managed at such times in the past without the love and care shown by family and/or friends. We were convinced that most old people want to remain in their own home and that frequently not enough is done to help them do so. It is easier to put them into an old people's home, even when this is not essential. We knew of cases of neglect, stealing from residents, and abuse in such homes. It is common knowledge that moving into a home, unless it is an exceptionally caring one and provides interesting activities, leads to deepening depression, mental decline, states of disorientation and confusion. Might confusion be a way of escaping from full awareness of what one has lost and is losing?

We spoke about the wish to be, at least some of the time, in the company of younger people. We found ourselves feeling inwardly young quite a lot of the time. On the other hand, the onset of a chronic illness or disability could make one suddenly feel years older. Even recovering from an operation took much longer than before. Some of us felt that we were sometimes made to feel old by being segregated, put at a table for the "oldies" at social gatherings or not included in young people's conversations. Perhaps it is hard for young people to realise that a person in their seventies, eighties, nineties and beyond may still be active and have an alert mind; that they are interested in the present, in new discoveries, in young people's ideals, even in sex, and may be enthused by beauty. We may in fact appreciate some things more than before. Since finding walking more difficult, I have, for instance, suddenly become more aware of, and enjoy watching, the delightful way little children move their feet and legs as they toddle or skip along. We bemoaned the fact that little consideration is given in Western society to how enriching it can be for young and old to mix and learn from each other. I look back with great pleasure at my stay in a Quaker college during my time of studying at university. It accommodated adults whose ages ranged from their late teens to their eighties. We helped and supported each other, had fun together, were stimulated and enlivened by each other's experiences as well as by differing reactions to what was happening in the world.

Members of the group acknowledged having less energy. Everything required more effort than before: shopping, preparing meals, sorting papers, having guests to stay, although that was such a pleasure. We had sometimes to give ourselves a push to get enough exercise or go out, especially in the evening. We were frustrated at being slower, unable to accomplish as much as in bygone days, needing more rest as well as sometimes feeling in too low a state to do much, while at the same time being acutely conscious of time and our lives slipping away. Someone mentioned being irritated and more upset by little things. It made me think of getting quite panicky when I mislay something, afraid that I must have lost it. Such minor mishaps set off fears about bigger issues: losing one's memory, one's mind disintegrating. We spoke about restrictions imposed on us by loss of motor ability: not able to run for the bus, drive a car, not able to walk far, fly, or undertake long journeys. We had, as far as possible, to find alternative ways of managing but also had to accept and be sad that we would never again be able to engage in some of the activities that had in the past provided so much pleasure; in my case, not being able to play my beloved cello, not being able to ski, having to avoid high altitudes, and missing being in the mountains I love. We admitted to, at times, feeling envious of those who were young and fit enough to follow such pursuits.

The will to go on and struggle with whatever limitations old age imposes brought to my mind the true story I had read of a lone mountaineer who, with great courage and determination, cut off part of his left arm which was stuck in the ice, as this was the only way to keep alive and continue on his path down the mountain. Similarly, if we are not to get stuck, we have to accept cutting ourselves off from many things we could do before, accept inevitable losses, however painful, and make the most of the life that is still available to us.

Some of our group felt that being old had its compensations: it was easier, for instance, to give oneself permission to have a nap after lunch, to watch television during day-time, even to do nothing without feeling unduly guilty. They felt they could allow themselves such freedom, no longer being admonished by parents for being lazy or wasting time. It made us aware of the demands we had, in the past, made on our parents, not sufficiently allowing them time to rest and enjoy their leisure time.

The question of where one felt at home, where we felt we belonged, was an important issue. Some spoke with nostalgia of having felt held, in their childhood and youth, within a closely-knit family, a good school or work environment and social network. This was thought to be to some extent replaced by having children and grandchildren. But the need to belong and be contained extended to being part of a social group: it could be a group of friends, a group based on shared interests; the warmth and care of a religious community with which most members were associated was mentioned as being of immense importance.

For many in our group, tracing their roots had become an important task. Some had travelled to places where their mothers and fathers had lived, had tried to find people who had known their parents, had visited the graves of grandparents and other family members. Some had become interested in genealogy, engaged in constructing a family tree, going back many generations; engaged also in writing family history and the story of their own lives. Those who had missed the chance to ask their elders questions about the past, and those whose parents had refused to talk about the painful as well as the joyful events in their lives, harboured deep regrets that all such knowledge was lost forever. We discovered that we all had the experience of owning old photographs, some of them inherited, but being unable to identify the people pictured. All these activities seemed to indicate an urge to place oneself within the generational chain, to know about one's forebears, internalise the past, and the wish to preserve such knowledge for the coming generation. There was a great desire to pass on family values and traditions. Great concern was felt that some of these were already being infringed by one's children and/or grandchildren and there was a fear that they might be lost altogether after one had gone. But how could we ensure that what we treasured was preserved without imposing our views, invading our offspring's freedom to develop their own style of life and learn from their experience?

Throughout our four meetings, serious thought had been interspersed with lighter moments. It was recognised that while a sense of humour was a great asset, joking at times also provided a necessary escape from too much emotional pain. The latter was particularly evident when we touched upon the subject of death. It seemed possible for everyone to accept the idea of mortality but thinking about the actual process of slowly dying raised acute fears of suffering unbearable physical pain, getting into states of panic, being overcome by catastrophic anxiety. We hoped, but were not at all sure, that we would have the courage and inner strength to bear whatever we might have to suffer. What came to my mind at this point in our discussion was the courage shown by an explorer who undertook the arduous and dangerous journey to the North Pole all on his own, though in radio communication with a support group. My associations clearly show that, even with support, I was visualising approaching death as an extremely challenging journey which one has ultimately to undertake on one's own.

We wondered about the nature of the difficulties we might encounter before we died and how we would be able to deal with them. It led to the question of whether there was anything we could do to prepare ourselves. Apart from practical matters such as making a will (or updating it) and sorting out one's finances—which everyone thought important but was reluctant to do—we all felt the wish to part in a loving way from those we knew. This involved looking at severed relationships, thinking about whom we had hurt, neglected, or been hurt by and had not forgiven. It meant trying to repair relationships in as far as it lay within our power to do so: overcoming long-harboured resentments, trying to forgive, asking to be forgiven, showing our love—and thus parting in peace.

While we cannot know how we shall cope with dying, it was felt that we could try to prepare ourselves spiritually. This spiritual journey had for many started long ago; for some in childhood, for some in adolescence, for many in mid-life. For some it was something that had lain dormant for a long time but was now returned to; for others, it was only now that it had become an urgent matter. The paths chosen to enhance the spiritual side of our nature took various forms. Some found it through participation in religious services and studies of religious texts; others, though not believing in a personal God, in prayer; some in trusting some loving creative force; for quite a few through meditation. All these were felt to be ways of getting in touch with some part within ourselves that connected us with the ongoing process of life and creativity beyond the self. It meant accepting at one and the same time our personal significance in contributing to the welfare of others (as well as to the environment) and our insignificance within this huge, expanding, evolving universe. This link to life beyond the self provides moments of hope at being able to attain the strength to accept and endure whatever the end of our life might bring. It makes it possible, at times, to attain tranquillity in the midst of outer and inner turmoil.

What is this turmoil? Is it a protest against having to give up life, greedily asking, like one of my patients: If there is death at the end, what is the point of living? Are we raging against fate, against those who are felt to be insufficiently caring, as Shakespeare so movingly demonstrates in the tragedy of King Lear. The feeling of catastrophic anxiety in the face of decline and death can so easily lead to us demanding attention from others, complaining that they do not care enough, don't show enough love. And if they don't, we may turn against them, punish them, rob them of their freedom and happiness. Such attacks in the outer and inner world may result in being thrown into the wilderness where hatred and persecution reign, falling into despair, descending into madness, unable to distinguish good from bad, truth from lies, raging against fate and God or alternatively feeling punished for our sins. Yet when there is someone strong and understanding enough, still showing tender care and love, like Lear's daughter Cordelia, faith in goodness makes helplessness and pain more bearable and may open the way to a more loving relationship.

We have a choice: avoid or face our fear of suffering and death. Far from taking us away from ordinary life, merging us with an ideal object, and providing an oceanic experience, as Freud thought, spiritual intouchness inspires awe at the mystery of life, greater awareness and appreciation of what we encounter everyday: the scent of flowers, the glorious autumn colours, the moving clouds, sunset, dawn, the song of birds; it enables us to feel connected to all that has life in it and be glad that it will continue after we have gone. Consideration of our finite life can urge us on to make the most of the time available to us. I cannot remember a time in my adult life when I was not aware of the words of the 90th Psalm: "Teach us to number our days".

I remember how even as a five-year-old I was very aware of death and its inevitability; the fact that there was no escape from it left me feeling terrified. (As I am writing, it occurs to me that it might have been the way my mother was affected by the death of her mother, after whom I was named, that made me so scared at that time.) The fear of dying is ever present, right from infancy, although we may repress it for much of the time. I remember asking my mother to save me from war and death; she had to promise to do so before I would go to sleep. What an impossible demand! My father tried to allay my fears by saying that I might be less afraid when I was a grown-up and that in his experience most people died peacefully.

I am impressed by Donald Winnicott and agree with his saying: "Oh God! May I be alive when I die" (cited in C. Winnicott, 1989). My father was like that. A few days before his ninety-fourth birthday, in full possession of his mind (never afraid of death, in spite of his experiences in World War One and the concentration camp), he had a philosophical discussion on "the meaning of time" with a friend who had phoned. Within moments of putting down the phone, he was gone, his heart just stopped. What a blessed life and a good way to die. Unlike him, I am sure my mother was afraid of death. She was full of vitality even when her strength ebbed away. I feared that she would fight against death and that there would be an agonising struggle at the end. But during the last six weeks of her life, I noticed a change, an acceptance of death. As she woke from sleep, she seemed sometimes to be talking to my father who had passed away many years before. She just slipped away, with my sister and I holding her hands, telling her we were right beside her. I feel deep gratitude at her having died so peacefully.

I have no experience of analysing very old patients, unlike Segal (1958) who was able to help an old man with his fear of death. I have, however, seen very elderly people for a few consultative sessions. In the majority of cases, the fact that they could share their thoughts and felt helped to understand the nature of their anxieties, brought considerable relief.

It was Mrs. A.'s daughter who suggested that her mother should come to see me. She was a pleasant-looking, nearly ninety-two-year-old lady who managed to come up the stairs to my consulting room in spite of her severe arthritis. She told me that she sometimes had attacks of pain that made her terrified of not being able to move. Asked about her family, she said her children were wonderfully kind and helped with shopping and visits to the doctor. They often invited her for meals although she was able to cook and bake for herself. When I encouraged her to tell me about her background, I learnt that she had come to England just before the outbreak of World War Two. Her sister had survived in Norway. This sister was described as being a very difficult person, aggressive and forever quarrelling with her parents and her siblings. Four years earlier this sister was found to have cancer; it had been diagnosed too late for her to benefit from treatment and she had died some months later. Mrs. A. told me that she found herself thinking of her often these days and of the pain she must have suffered. She paused and remained silent. I remarked on her having fallen silent and asked whether she could tell me more about her relationship with her sister. Mrs. A. said that she had been thinking how lonely her sister must have felt, cut off from the family. I asked whether she had visited her. "No,", she said, "I didn't." She went on to say that she now feels that in spite of their strained relationship, she ought to have gone to see her. I said she seemed to regret that she had not done so and seemed to feel guilty about this. After a further silence, I ventured to say that she had described the recurring pains and inability to move as "attacks"; maybe she felt that it was her sister attacking her, causing her such pain as she had suffered and making Mrs. A. as inert as her dead self. Mrs. A. pondered what I had said and then told me that the idea that her panic was linked to her sister had not occurred to her but she would think about it.

At our second meeting a week later Mrs. A. told me that she still had episodes of feeling she cannot move but she had not got into any further states of panic. Her daughter had asked her to come with her and her family for a holiday in France. Her doctor said she was fit enough to travel but she was too frightened to leave home, afraid she might again have panic attacks if she went abroad. We established that she would be with her family and within reach of good medical care if the need for it arose. I then spoke about travelling being perhaps quite especially linked to her guilt at not having travelled to see her sister when she was alive; and hence perhaps she feared that she would be punished by having an attack of panic and would die if she went on holiday abroad. Mrs. A. thought for a while and, looking sad, said my words made sense.

I was very happy to learn that she did go abroad with her daughter's family and when she returned, she let me know that although she had been at times anxious, she had been able to enjoy much of her trip.

Mrs. B. also came to see me at the suggestion of her daughter. The latter was concerned at her mother having given up almost all social life. A neat, smartly dressed but extremely worried-looking lady of eighty-six, Mrs. B. immediately told me she could not go out any more, neither to the University of the Third Age nor to a discussion group for seniors where current political issues were debated. Her memory had lately got so much worse that sometimes she could not find the right words to express what she wanted to say, had to stop in mid-sentence because her mind went blank. I said she seemed to be terrified of losing her mind and asked whether she had spoken to her doctor about it. She told me that she had and that the doctor had reassured her that her degree of memory-loss was not uncommon at her age and was nothing to worry about. I said she appeared to be extremely worried all the same. I got the feeling she was afraid that others in the group would notice her being lost for words. She said that was it, everyone would know and they would talk about her and tell others in her social circle. I said she seemed to regard her problem as something to be very ashamed of. I asked about how she spent her time at home. She told me that she is very house-proud and is busy with keeping her home clean and tidy. She loved to see her grandchildren but they made such a mess, it upset her. She also read a great deal and kept up with current affairs. Thinking about her very neat appearance and her emphasis on order and cleanliness, I wondered whether she needed everything, including herself, to be perfect (in an obsessional way). Maybe this made it impossible to accept that her memory was not as good as before, which is inevitable as one gets older. I wondered whether it was her own non-acceptance of her mental imperfection that led her to believe others would be critical and not respect her; she even seemed to fear they would laugh at her losing her memory and take pleasure in gossiping about her. Surely, I said, there were others in this group of senior citizens who had age-related problems of one sort or another. I also pointed out that she had not had any difficulty in talking to me. She said she would think about what I had said and we fixed another appointment for the following week.

At our second meeting, she told me that the leader of the discussion group had written to her, saying she hoped Mrs. B. would come back soon. In spite of this, Mrs. B. told me: "I have definitely decided not to go there any more, I am not going to risk making a fool of myself." It was too shameful and she was sure people would tell others and so she would lose all her friends. I said it seemed such a pity to withdraw from something that she obviously enjoyed. Perhaps her anxiety about not finding the right words contributed to her mind going blank. I said it seemed to me that we needed to think some more about her feeling so intolerant of any shortcomings. She was treating her problem with disdain rather than with compassion and feared that others would be equally critical and contemptuous.

She was quiet and seemed to be thoughtful but then sat up, holding herself very straight and told me that she had made up her mind not to go back to any group and there was also no point in coming to see me again. I said I felt very sorry that she felt talking with me to be pointless. She repeated that she did not want to see me again. I said I was sorry not to have been able to help her. I would, of course, be very ready to meet with her again if she changed her mind. Or, if she preferred to see someone else, I could give her the name of another therapist. I told her that I felt it was important for her to have help. Her fear of others treating her loss of memory with the same disdain as herself was making her lead a restricted life and that was such a big loss.

I considered Mrs. B. to be at breaking point, depressed and persecuted, as her perfectionism, her feeling in control of her physical and mental powers, could no longer be maintained. I was very worried about her. Without breaking confidentiality, I decided to speak to her daughter, saying I was worried and asking her to encourage her mother to continue to get ongoing therapeutic treatment.

Bion pointed out that a breakdown can be a break-through. In the above case, the break-through of looking at and bearing the painful truth of signs of ageing would be more realistic and healthy than feelings of shame and persecution. Mrs. B.'s anxieties are likely to increase. I fear that she will become increasingly depressed, persecuted and isolated. If she could be helped to accept and mourn her losses, she could attain greater emotional strength and be capable of a richer life.

Mr. C., aged seventy-five, said that it was Mrs. A. who had recommended him to come to see me. He told me that he was extremely upset. His grandson had been involved in a car accident and though the ambulance was called for and came quickly, the doctors could not save him. He was severely brain-damaged and died within a few days. Mr. C. was hardly able to hold back his tears; he apologised. I said it was alright to cry, offered him paper handkerchiefs and when he became calmer, asked when the accident had happened. "It was three months ago but it feels like yesterday," Mr. C. said. "Actually I feel even worse now than when I first had this dreadful news."

I asked Mr. C. to tell me about his grandson. I learnt that Tony was twenty-three, intelligent, had a very loving nature, and had many friends. Since leaving university, he had often come to help Mr. C. with his gardening and to teach him to use the computer. Mr. C. spoke for some time about his beloved grandson and then told me that Tony had taken a degree in business studies. He went on to say that his own father had designed clothes and built up a firm that was well-known for the quality of its products and the reasonable prices he charged his customers. Mr. C. had helped his father and eventually taken over as managing director of the firm. Mr. C's children and granddaughters had other interests but Tony had been helping him at work and had enjoyed it. Mr. C. had hoped that he would, in time, be ready to run the family business. "But now there is no one to hand it over to, it feels like the end of the line, with the family firm's name lost forever," he said. Mr. C. was again in tears.

We sat in silence for a few minutes and I then said: "It seems that this grandson was the joy of your old age and great hope was invested in him. As well as missing him and mourning his death, you are telling me that he was to have continued to keep the family firm running and that now there will be no one to keep the firm's name alive. So Tony's death also brings back to your mind the loss of your father and what he achieved. And there is the approaching death of the family firm that you have spent your life building up further and are not able to hand on. I think you are feeling all these losses and this makes it so utterly unbearable." Mr. C. nodded and we sat in silence until the end of the session. We shook hands at parting, having arranged to meet again a fortnight later.

When I saw him next, Mr. C. said he had cried less at home but felt very upset right now, though it was good to be able to talk about his grief; his son and his family were suffering and he did not feel he could burden them further by talking about his own feelings. I suggested it might actually be helpful for everyone to share their precious memories of the boy they loved. I added that it must be very hard for him not to meet with the family and Tony's friends although I could see that his particular concern about the firm was his private affair. Mr. C. said Tony had brought some of his friends to his house and they used to have fun together; maybe he could try to keep in touch with them.

I saw Mr. C. a third time. He felt very sad but was trying to accept that he would need to sell the family firm when he was no longer able to manage the work. He told me that he had been seeing more of his family and had invited two of Tony's close friends to his house. These had been very emotional meetings but it had been good to share memories and feel that Tony remained alive in all their minds.

It seems to be typical of the elderly that they tend not to seek therapeutic help unless someone else encourages them to do so. I wonder why this should be? Do they feel that they are not worth it or think they are too old to be helped by talking to a therapist about what worries them? Reaching old age and facing the end of our life evokes earlier, undigested, primitive anxieties related to loss. Such stirrings in the unconscious often bring with them a receptiveness to explore the meaning of the emotional pain in depth.

REFERENCES

Abraham, K. (1924). A short study of the development of the libido, viewed in the light of mental disorders. In: *Selected Papers on Psycho-Analysis*. London: Hogarth Press, 1927; repr, London: Karnac, 1979.

Alvarez, A. (1992). *Live Company: Psychoanalytic Psychotherapy with Autistic, Borderline, Deprived and Abused Children*. London: Routledge.

Bick, E. (1968). The experience of the skin in early object relations. *International Journal of Psycho-Analysis, 49*: 484–486. Also in: Harris, M. & Bick, E. (1987) *Collected Papers of Martha Harris and Esther Bick.*, Strath Tay: Clunie Press.

Bion, W. R. (1962a). *Learning from Experience*. London: Heinemann.

Bion, W. R. (1962b). A theory of thinking. *International Journal of Psycho-Analysis, 43*: 306–310. Also in: *Second Thoughts: Selected Papers on Psycho-Analysis*. London: Heinemann; repr. London: Karnac, 1984.

Bion, W. R. (1970). *Attention and Interpretation*. London: Tavistock; repr, London: Karnac, 1988.

Bowlby, J. (1969). *Attachment and Loss, Vol. 1: Attachment*. New York: Basic Books.

Bowlby, J. (1973). *Attachment and Loss, Vol. 2: Separation, Anxiety and Anger*. New York: Basic Books.

Bowlby, J. (1980). *Attachment and Loss, Vol. 3: Loss, Sadness and Depression*. New York: Basic Books.

Coleridge, S. T. (1811–12). On the nature of love in *Romeo and Juliet*. In: R. A. Foakes (Ed.), *Coleridge's Criticism of Shakespeare: A Selection*. London: Athlone, 1989.

Dubinsky, A. (2010). The musings of babies: Reflective thinking, emotion and the re-integration of the good object. *International Journal of Infant Observation, 13*, 1: 5–13. Also in: Magagna, J. (Ed.) *The Silent Child: Communication Without Words*. London: Karnac, 2012.

Freud, A. (1966). *Normality and Pathology in Childhood: Assessments of Development*. London: Hogarth Press; repr, London: Karnac 1980.

Freud, S. (1917). Mourning and Melancholia. *S. E., 14*. London: Hogarth Press.

Freud, S. (1920). Beyond the Pleasure Principle. *S. E., 18*.

Grier, F. (2006). Reflections on the phenomenon of adoration in relationships, both human and divine. In: D. M. Black (Ed.), *Psychoanalysis and Religion in the 21st Century: Competitors or collaborators?* London: Routledge.

Keats, J. *Letters of John Keats*, R. Gittings (Ed.). Oxford: OUP, 1987.

Klein, M. (1940). Mourning and its relation to manic-depressive states. In: *Love, Guilt and Reparation and Other Works, 1921–1945*. London: Hogarth Press, 1975.

Klein, M. (1957). Envy and gratitude. In: *Envy and Gratitude and Other Works, 1946–1963*. London: Hogarth Press, 1975.

Maiello, S. (1995). The sound object: A hypothesis about prenatal auditory experience and memory. *Journal of Child Psychotherapy, 21*, 1: 23–41.

Meltzer, D. (1988). The aesthetic conflict. In: *The Apprehension of Beauty*. Strath Tay: Clunie Press.

Music, G. (2011). *Nurturing Natures: Attachment and Children's Emotional, Sociocultural and Brain Development*. Hove: Psychology Press.

Nehru, J. (1950). *Independence and After: A Collection of Speeches, 1946–1949*. New York: John Day.

Phillips, A. (1999). *Saying No: Why It's Important for You and Your Child*. London: Faber & Faber.

Piontelli, A. (1992). *From Fetus to Child: An observational and psychoanalytic study*. London: Tavistock/Routledge.

Prechtl, H. F. R. (1989). Fetal behaviour. In: A. Hill & J. Volpe (Eds.). *Fetal Neurology*. New York: Raven Press.

Reid, S. (Ed.) (1997). *Developments in Infant Observation: The Tavistock Model*. London: Routledge.

Robertson, J. (1952). *A Two-year-old Goes to Hospital* (Film). Extract available at http://www.youtube.com/watch?v=Fl1 scJ3ZwOE

Salzberger-Wittenberg, I. (1978). The use of "here and now" experiences in a teaching conference on psychotherapy as a means of gaining insight into the nature of the helping relationship. *Journal of Child Psychotherapy, 4, 4*: 33–50. Also in: P. S. Barrows (Ed.), *Key Papers from the Journal of Child Psychotherapy*. Hove: Brunner-Routledge, 2004.

Salzberger-Wittenberg, I., Williams, G. & Osborne, E. (1983). *The Emotional Experience of Learning and Teaching*. London: Routledge & Kegan Paul; repr, London: Karnac, 1999.

Segal, H. (1957). Notes on symbol formation. *International Journal of Psycho-Analysis, 75*: 611–618. Also in: E. B. Spillius (Ed.), *Melanie Klein Today, Vol 1: Mainly Theory*. London: Routledge, 1988.

Segal, H. (1958). Fear of death - notes on the analysis of an old man. *International Journal of Psycho-Analysis, 39*: 178–181. Also in: Junkers, G. (Ed.) (2006), *Is it Too Late? Key papers on psychoanalysis and ageing*. London: Karnac.

Shakespeare, W. *As You Like It*. In: *The Arden Shakespeare edition of the works of William Shakespeare*. London: Routledge, 1989; *King Lear*. In: *The Arden Shakespeare edition of the works of William Shakespeare*. London: Routledge, 1972.

Steiner, J. (1993). *Psychic Retreats: Pathological Organizations in Psychotic, Neurotic and Borderline Patients*. London: Routledge.

Tomatis, A. A. (1981). *La nuit utérine*. Paris: Editions Stock.

Waddell, M. (1998). *Inside Lives: Psychoanalysis and the Growth of the Personality*. London: Duckworth; repr, London: Karnac, 2002.

Williams, G. (1997). Double deprivation. In: *Internal Landscapes and Foreign Bodies: Eating Disorders and other Pathologies*. London: Duckworth; repr, London: Karnac, 2002.

Winnicott, C. (1989). D. W. W.: A reflection. In: Winnicott, D. W. edited by C. Winnicott, R. Shepherd and M. Davis. *Psycho-Analytic Explorations*. London: Karnac.

Winnicott, D. W. (1949). Birth memories, birth trauma and anxiety. In: *Collected Papers: Through Paediatrics to Psychoanalysis*. London: Tavistock (1958); repr, London: Karnac, 1992.

Winnicott, D. W. (1953). Transitional objects and transitional phenomena: A study of the first not-me possession. *International Journal of Psycho-Analysis, 34*: 89–97.

Winnicott, D. W. (1971). *Playing and Reality*. London: Tavistock.

BIBLIOGRAPHY

Bion, W. R. (1965). *Transformations*. London: Karnac.

Bion, W. R. (1967). *Second Thoughts: Selected Papers on Psycho-Analysis*.: Heinemann; repr, London: Karnac, 1984.

Eliot, T. S. (1943). *Four Quartets*. New York: Harcourt, Brace.

Raphael-Leff, J. (1993). *Pregnancy: The Inside Story*. London: Karnac.

Symington, N. (1994). *Emotion and Spirit: Questioning the Claims of Psychoanalysis and Religion*. London: Cassell; repr, London: Karnac, 1998.

INDEX